humOR
for the holidays

Stories, Quips, and Quotes
for Thanksgiving,
Christmas, and New Year's

humOR
for the holidays

HOWARD BOOKS
A DIVISION OF SIMON & SCHUSTER
New York   London   Toronto   Sydney

Jack Hayford • Patsy Clairmont • Martha Bolton • Tim Wildmon
Lynn Bowen Walker • Charlene Ann Baumbich • and many more

Our purpose at Howard Books is to:
- *Increase faith* in the hearts of growing Christians
- *Inspire holiness* in the lives of believers
- *Instill hope* in the hearts of struggling people everywhere
Because He's coming again!

Published by Howard Books, a division of Simon & Schuster, Inc.
1230 Avenue of the Americas, New York, NY 10020
www.howardpublishing.com

Humor for the Holidays © 2006 by Howard Books

10 Digit ISBN: : 1-58229-582-4   13 Digit ISBN: 9781582295824
Library of Congress Cataloging-in-Publication Data
Humor for the holidays / compiled by Shari MacDonald ; illustrated by Dennis Hill.
    p.   cm.
    Summary: "compilation of holiday stories—Provided by publisher.
    Includes bibliographical references.
    ISBN-13: 978-1-58229-583-1 (hardcover)
    ISBN-10: 1-58229-583-2 (hardcover)
1. Christmas. 2. Holidays—Humor. I. MacDonald, Shari, II. Hill, Dennis
BV45.H86   2006
818'.5402080334—dc22   2006024687

10 9 8 7 6 5 4 3 2 1

For information regarding special discounts for bulk purchases, please contact Simon & Schuster Special Sales at 1-800-456-6798 or business@simonandschuster.com.

Edited by Jennifer Stair
Cover design by Dennis Hill
Interior Design by Inside Out Design & Typesetting
Cover art and illustrations by Dennis Hill

Unless otherwise noted, Scripture quotations are taken from the HOLY BIBLE, NEW INTERNATIONAL VERSION®. Copyright © 1973, 1978, 1984 by International Bible Society. Used by permission of Zondervan Publishing House. All rights reserved. Scriptures marked NASB are taken from the NEW AMERICAN STANDARD BIBLE®. Copyright © 1960, 1962, 1963, 1968, 1971, 1972, 1973, 1975, 1977, 1995 by The Lockman Foundation. Used by permission. Scriptures marked NKJV are from the NEW KING JAMES VERSION®. Copyright © 1979, 1980, 1982, 1983, Thomas Nelson, Inc., Publishers. Used by permission.

Editorial Note: Mistakes in grammar and punctuation that were inherent in the original source were not corrected.

Thank you, publishers and authors who granted us permission to reprint the stories in this book. In a few cases, we were unable to determine the original author. If you are one of those authors, please contact us by writing to Howard Books, 3117 North 7th St., West Monroe, LA 71291-2227 and we will give you credit in future printings.

Contents

Chapter 1: Christmas Is Coming, Tra-La, Tra-La...

Chapter 2: The Chaos Theory of Christmas

Chapter 3:
The Gift of Christmas

Chapter 4:
Peas on Earth ... and Other Tasty Holiday Tidbits

Chapter 5:
The Spirit of Christmas

Chapter 6:
Until Next Year ...

Christmas Is Coming, Tra-La, Tra-La...

All I Want for Christmas
Is a Parking Place

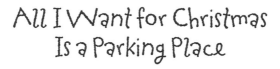

Dave Barry

Once again we find ourselves enmeshed in
the Holiday Season, that very special time
of year when we join with our loved ones
in sharing centuries-old traditions such as
trying to find a parking space at the mall.

The Best-Laid Plans

Karen Scalf Linamen

As we approach Thanksgiving, many of my friends are busy planning holiday dinners for their families. I tend to run behind on these things. I'm not thinking about Thanksgiving yet. How can I? I'm not done sewing the finishing touches on my five-year-old's Halloween costume.

The truth is, planning far enough in advance to defrost a pound of hamburger in time for dinner is a challenge for me. And when it comes to planning ahead for major holidays…well, I can't tell you how many turkeys I've defrosted in less than two hours using a blow-dryer.

But it's not like I NEVER plan ahead.

For example, there was the time I spent hours drawing up plans for a playhouse for our backyard. I used transparent

overlays for various construction phases, colored pencils to indicate different building materials, and a black marker to pinpoint every nail. The good news is that my architectural masterpiece has been put to good use. In fact, this very moment it's under my coffee cup, protecting the wood grain of my desk.

Then there was the time I planned to lose thirty pounds before summer. I lost five and discovered that you can really perk up the flavor of fat-free cookies with the simple addition of two scoops of Dreyers Rocky Road ice cream.

I have lots of really great plans. Sometimes I sit around and try to figure out what keeps me from turning a few more of them into reality.

Part of the problem is that I procrastinate.

Part of the problem is that I procrastinate.

For example, at this very moment, across from the desk where I'm writing, there is an empty wooden frame hanging on the wall. I hung it there with every intention of putting a picture in it the next day. That was two years ago.

I've heard there are support groups for this kind of thing. I keep meaning to find one.

My other problem is that I get distracted a lot. Like just now. I was busy writing this chapter when I decided I wanted to include a quote by Albert Einstein, something about the power of the imagination. Realizing the book containing the quote was in my bedroom, I ran upstairs. While I was upstairs, my husband phoned to remind me of our lunch

plans. Thinking of lunch, I decided to take a quick shower and change clothes. After I showered and dressed, I walked back into my office and sat at my computer and remembered the book. It was still in my bedroom.

Refusing to be undone, I headed back upstairs, thinking, "When I come back down I should bring the vacuum since the dog has been shedding in the den." I went directly to the closet, grabbed the vacuum, wrestled it down the stairs, deposited it in the den, then returned to my desk. It wasn't until I sat down and faced my computer that I remembered the book. Still in my bedroom. Still upstairs.

You'll just have to take my word about that quote. It was a good one.

And when I'm not forgetting to plan…or making a plan and then putting it off…or making plans and then getting distracted, I'm having my life planned out for me by my kids.

Which may not be such a bad thing.

One morning when Kacie was four, I was getting her dressed when she said, "Mom, if you worked at a circus, could you take me to work with you?"

"Sure. I'm sure I could arrange that."

"Then stop writing. You need to work for a circus. Can you buy a job at a circus?"

I laughed. "Not exactly. But maybe we could find some reason for them to hire me. I know, I could feed the animals! Wanna help me feed the animals?"

"Okay. But not the lions. Only the nice animals. Like the goats."

Of course. After all, what circus would be complete without goats?

So Kacie has my career all planned out for me. And to tell the truth, it's a nice feeling.

You know who else is in the process of making plans for me and for you as well? I'll give you a hint. He's the author of these powerful words: "For I know the plans I have for you," declares the LORD, "plans to prosper you and not to harm you, plans to give you hope and a future" (Jer. 29:11).

It's so easy to rush about in a self-induced lather! Indeed, a hefty chunk of my life is spent making plans, breaking plans, and recovering from plans of mine that have gone awry. Perhaps I'd do well to remember that, ultimately, my well-being rests not in the plans of my making, but in the hands of my Maker. Best yet, his plans for me are better than mine could ever be!

Of course, I'm not saying you and I should NEVER make plans. After all, as I write this, Thanksgiving is merely days away and those turkeys don't exactly defrost themselves.

This year, I think I'm going to change my ways. No more last-minute scrambling for me. I'm actually going to plan ahead.

I've already moved my blow-dryer into the kitchen.

Thanksgiving Rolls Around, and So Do the Dishes

Marti Attoun

That grandest meal on wheels, Thanksgiving, will park at my table this year.

In our family, everyone hauls in a dish. Crisscrossing the countryside on laps and floorboards, and in shallow boxes, Tupperware, and lidless bowls with dishtowels for covers, will be all our family favorites.

The dishes vary according to road and passenger conditions, but the menu always includes Overly Tossed Salad, Crammed Corn, Cranberry Slosh, Raked Beans, Footprint Pie, Defiled Eggs, and assorted Casserolings.

The Footprint Pie will be a berry, pumpkin, or pecan.

They all look alike after a restless kid gets bored with balancing it on his knees and plops it on the floorboard.

Crammed Corn is another must-have. During the first jostle of its journey in a casserole dish on the back seat, wedged between the hot rolls and oyster dressing, the Crammed Corn starts to slip and slurp. By the time it arrives on the table, there are just a couple of clods left. But the hot rolls are super-moist.

Our Thanksgiving fare always includes Defiled Eggs. A starving passenger can't resist snatching just one of the yellow middles. Then just one more.

> By the time the cake lands on the table, the frosting will have more dents than the turkey on the day after Thanksgiving.

The potholders can't keep their mitts off the homemade cakes, either. I was a young potholder once, so I know how "just a little lick" to waylay starvation turns into dips and dives along the sides of the cake where it won't immediately be visible. By the time the cake lands on the table, the frosting will have more dents than the turkey on the day after Thanksgiving.

Our cornucopia always runneth over with Raked Beans with limp bacon surfing on top, Picked-on Pickles, Squashed Yellow Squash, and Bandied Yams.

It wouldn't look, sound, or taste like Thanksgiving, though, without these well-traveled dishes and their tales. We laugh about potholes and potholders. Then we give thanks for a Relished Tray and all those responsible.

A Thanksgiving Recipe

G. Ron Darbee

It amazes me to realize how many of my memories are tied to food, although a look in the mirror puts the pieces of the puzzle in place. The sight of a certain pastry in the bakery window sends me decades back; I find myself, once again, holding my father's hand and begging for a dime. One bite of cinnamon toast and I'm sitting at the kitchen table too sick to attend school, but not quite sick enough to forego my mother's coddling. And turkey? That takes me back to my grandmother's house.

As best I can recall, my grandmother's kitchen contained a large, stainless steel oven and absolutely nothing else. I'll admit I probably missed a few things, but for the life of me, I don't remember anything besides that beautiful, shiny, warm

oven. Sure, she probably owned a toaster or a blender—a refrigerator at the very least. If so, they escape me as minor tools of an artist whose masterpiece was created in another medium.

Thanksgiving at Grandma's was a Darbee family tradition, and members gathered from the four corners of the world: Brooklyn, Queens, and the north and south shores of Long Island. Aunts and uncles, cousins of the first and second variety, everyone with a remote connection to my father's side was invited and duty bound to attend. Of course, marriages and various ties required some to make only a brief appearance between obligations, but their expressed regrets were undoubtedly heartfelt and sincere. Grandma's house was, without question, the place to be.

Dinner at Grandma's was less a meal than an event. Mashed potatoes and gravy, little gherkin pickles—I always got yelled at for sneaking them from the table before we were officially called to dinner—cranberry sauce, candied yams, and beets—thought to be poisonous, they caused me no temptation whatsoever—were but a few of the many accompaniments to the holiday fare. A juicy, pink ham always graced the table, and a turkey, dark brown and cooked to perfection, was the star attraction. Oh yeah, and rolls. Grandma always made fresh rolls; she wouldn't have dreamed of popping them from a can. A selection of pumpkin, apple, and cherry pies served to motivate the younger, more picky members in the digestion of the aforementioned beets.

The perfect meal certainly wasn't our only Thanksgiving tradition. Serving the meal several hours later than promised ran a close second. Each year, family members received

explicit instructions to arrive no later than one o'clock because dinner would be served precisely at two. Apparently, Grandma claimed Matthew 25:13, "Therefore keep watch, because you do not know the day or the hour," and applied it rather liberally. By three o'clock most of us kids began to get fidgety, and by four, talk of revolt started spreading through the house. When dinner was finally served, sometime in December, I think, the group set about the meal as if ending a forty-day fast.

My cousins and I used this time to take part in yet another time-honored tradition, namely roughhousing, troublemaking, and beating each other senseless. My father and his three siblings were responsible for eight offspring, with not a single "Y" chromosome among them. Eight boys under any one roof are bound to create havoc, and we were never a group to fall short of expectations. Having my bottom warmed—a term that sounds more pleasant, but still means whopped or standing with my nose in the corner for some length of time was part of that tradition I remember somewhat less fondly.

It wasn't until I married and joined the Marine Corps that I realized how much these traditions meant to me. With more than two thousand miles separating us from our families, Thanksgiving during the early years of our marriage was a quiet and understated affair. Like most young military couples, we didn't have much money. Traveling home for a weekend was so far beyond our budget that it wasn't worthy of consideration. A frozen turkey roll, canned corn, and refrigerator biscuits were the extent of our holiday feast. We both felt something was missing, though good judgment

restrained me from saying exactly what, and we began to view Thanksgiving as just another paid holiday.

Then one year in early November, sitting in the living room with a pair of couples we considered our closest friends, someone suggested we pool our resources and put together an "old-fashioned" Thanksgiving dinner. "The kind my Grandma used to make," somebody suggested. I couldn't have agreed more.

"Why not?" I said, and everyone seemed to agree all at once. Sue volunteered to make pies, someone else signed up for the vegetables, and we all chipped in for a twenty-pound turkey. We started to get excited, and I decided to call home and get my grandmother's recipe for the world's most perfect turkey.

"Grandma," I said into the phone, "can you give me your recipe for Thanksgiving turkey?" The anticipation in my voice was drowned out by the sound of my stomach rumbling.

"Oh, I don't even know what I do," she said. "There's usually a set of instructions on the bag with the bird. Mine always comes out too dry, anyway. Just don't trust those little pop-up thermometers," she continued. "I've never seen one that worked worth a lick."

"Come on, Grandma," I pleaded. "You always make the best turkey. Don't you have some kind of a secret, something you add or do to make it come out just right?"

"It seems to me," Grandma said, "that you've never had a turkey I didn't cook, so I doubt you have much to compare it to." She made a point I had previously failed to consider. "But as it turns out," she said, "I do have a few secrets I'd be willing to share."

"Get yourself a turkey," she continued, "and surround it with the people you love and care about the most. Cook it as slow as humanly possible to give everyone some time to enjoy each other's company, and thank God for every blessing in your lives. I promise you it will be the best Thanksgiving dinner you ever imagined."

"Get yourself a turkey, and surround it with the people you love and care about the most."

As we sat around the table that year—three young couples—far from our home and families, someone suggested that we join hands and share with the group the blessings we were most thankful for. Sue and I continue that tradition with our family to this day.

My grandmother's recipe turned out to be a huge success. That meal remains one of my all-time favorites, and the entire evening went off with only one hitch.

"What happened to all the gherkins?" Sue asked as we sat down to begin the dinner. "I put a whole plate of them on the table half an hour ago." She never did find those pickles. They just seemed to disappear. What a strange and unusual thing.

Who Needs Cookbooks When You've Got a Phone?

Marti Attoun

The latest power blender, electronic toaster, and remote-control grill are useful gadgets for some cooks, but my family couldn't cook without that basic: a phone.

When I get frisky in the kitchen and venture beyond store-bought pimento cheese, I call Mom or one of my sisters for detailed instructions. It took three phone calls before I could get my salmon cakes to cling together. If Mom's line had been busy any longer, we would have eaten salmon kibbles.

"Cooking by telephone" runs in my family. My Aunt Geraldine, who lives in Florida, once had a frantic call from

her daughter Mary in Baltimore.

"Mom, I bought this ground beef three days ago. Is it still safe to eat?" Mary asked.

"Cooking by telephone" runs in my family.

Her mother strained to see across several states and up the Eastern seaboard.

"Mary, if it's slug-colored and stinks, throw it out," her mother finally said.

When my niece Kirsten spent a semester away at school in England, it would have been much cheaper for her to eat out every meal than to attempt to cook, which required multiple phone calls. For Thanksgiving, Kirsten decided to fix a turkey for the other homesick American students, although she'd never fixed anything more complicated than cinnamon toast.

She called home, hysterical.

"The turkey's in the bathtub defrosting," she said. "What in the world do I do next?"

Step by step, her cooking coach talked her through the process, including plundering the bird's body cavity for its grab bag of giblets. Shrieks could be heard over the phone lines. The cooking lesson cost three times as much as the bird.

My husband, too, cooks by phone when he gets a sentimental hungering for one of his family's Mediterranean recipes. Thanks to a cordless, he's able to pluck the ingredients from the fridge and cabinet as his sister recites them. This means that he doesn't write down the recipe, so the next time he attempts boulettes, he calls again. It's a good excuse to

spend quality (that means priced by-the-minute) time with his siblings, though.

My daughter, who is away at college, called not long ago to ask how to soften a rock of brown sugar for chocolate chip cookies. I don't know why she didn't call her grandmother directly.

"Do you have a hammer?" I asked her. "Oh, wait. Let me call Granny and I'll call you back." Mom's advice of a minute in the microwave with a cup of water worked much better. We really needed a conference call for *that* cooking lesson.

When someone in the family hankers for an unusual recipe, Aunt Iris often gets a phone call because she keeps an inventory of 200 or so cookbooks.

For example, my brother-in-law Dan lusted for persimmon jelly, and Aunt Iris had the recipe. A couple of weeks ago, he itched for old-fashioned scrapple—and that's not something you find in the Pillsbury Bake-off cookbooks. Finally, he called Aunt Iris, who dipped into one of her Ozark cookbooks.

"First, boil up a hog's head," Aunt Iris said. "When you're finished, call me back for Step 2."

I hope Aunt Iris isn't still waiting by the phone.

On Wings Like Turkeys

Chris Fabry

Ever want to teach your children a lesson and learn something new yourself? It happened to me one Thanksgiving when my employer provided us with an extra twelve-pound bird. We decided to do the turkey tithe. *If nothing else, this would make Larry Burkett proud,* I thought. My wife had planned to take the older children to a food shelter in the late morning to help serve the hungry and needy. She sees this as a way to expose them to those who are less fortunate.

I had a better plan and questioned whether the shelter would actually need help. "On Thanksgiving and Christmas everyone shows up to help, and then they go away. They need volunteers the rest of the year, but people show up at

the holidays because it makes them feel good." Then I added the *coup de fowl*, "Not you of course, dear."

The addendum didn't work. The damage was done. To her credit, Andrea went anyway, later in the day.

The bigger question was not if she would go, but whether she would take our precious over-and-above turkey with her. Andrea had cooked it early in the morning, and it was crisp and brown by ten o'clock. She wanted to donate it to the shelter, but I believed we should do something "local."

"What do you suggest?" my wife asked. "Just go out and find someone who looks turkey deprived?"

"Nobody lives by faith anymore," I said. "If we really believed God, we'd pray he would lead us to the right person, and then we'd take that turkey and give it to them.

Andrea cried that day, though I didn't notice. "It takes every ounce of courage I have just to go to the shelter," she would say later. She felt defeated, but instead of fighting she said, "Okay, let's go."

It was pouring rain as we buckled the kids. The smell of wet leaves and fresh baked turkey filled the air.

"I'm hungry," someone said.

"Quiet kids, we're about to see God work."

I was as expectant as an overdue mother. I was sure something wondrous was about to happen. After all, I was praying to the God who made the sun stand still, who knocked down

> I was as expectant as an overdue mother. I was sure something wondrous was about to happen.

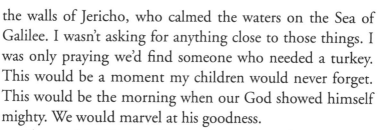

the walls of Jericho, who calmed the waters on the Sea of Galilee. I wasn't asking for anything close to those things. I was only praying we'd find someone who needed a turkey. This would be a moment my children would never forget. This would be the morning when our God showed himself mighty. We would marvel at his goodness.

The windshield wipers beat to the rhythm of some current Christian tune. A few obstinate leaves clung to the trees, but most were on the ground like a wet blanket. We drove past deserted parking lots and fast-food restaurants. A few cars shared the road with us. Absolutely no one walked the street.

"Dad?" someone called from the backseat. It is the shortest question in the English language which, being interpreted, means, "What in the world are we doing?"

"Pray, kids. I know we're going to find that one person. Look hard now. Don't give up."

We pulled into an apartment complex with its overflowing trash bins. I parked, the rain coming down even harder now, and scanned the rows of curtained windows. Nothing. Just the sound of the rain and the radio. I turned it off, half expecting someone to tap on the window and ask, "Sir, can you help a poor man find some food?"

A still, small voice broke the silence.

"Dad, there's nobody here."

Aimlessly we roamed, driving through foreign neighborhoods and alleys.

"How are they going to get the turkey home if it's raining so hard?" someone else asked.

"Maybe we'll give them a ride," I said.

"Dad, there's no more room. We take up all the seats."

"Are there no Joshuas or Calebs in this car?" I said. "You guys are worse than the children of Israel. You just wait and see."

But it was like waiting for the Great Pumpkin to rise from the patch. God had provided the ram in the thicket for Abraham. I had provided the turkeys in the pan. But where was Isaac or whoever was supposed to eat it?

Andrea looked at me and tried to smile. "Let me take it to the shelter; I'm sure they can use it. You go home and watch the game."

It felt like failure, but sometimes faith feels that way. Sometimes the right thing means obeying the call you've already been given, even if it wasn't your idea. Sometimes faith doesn't make you feel as good as you want. Faith can make you mount up with turkey wings.

I'm not sure my kids remember our fruitless search that day, but they have wonderful stories of serving hungry people and how thankful those at the shelter were for their help. I looked at Andrea's face later as we sat down to eat our own meal. There was satisfaction in it, as if a stone had been rolled away.

"How do you like your turkey?" she asked, wondering whether to serve me dark or white meat.

"Well done," I said, "Well done."

Fowl Play!
(How Not to Be a Turkey
at the Thanksgiving Table)

Marti Attoun

Come Thanksgiving, the grown-ups in my family will feast around the dining-room table while the not-yet-grown-ups sit at annexed card tables, coffee tables and the piano bench.

Every year someone whines, "No fair. When do I get to sit at the big table?" This year, I offer some guidelines about graduating to the "big table."

- The plate should remain bare until "amen" is uttered. Even then, "amen" does not mean "plunge in" and knock Aunt Louise into the relish tray while snatching a roll.

- You should know without asking that a cornucopia has nothing to do with Granny's bunion.

- When eating an olive, you should refrain from pretending it's a peashooter and aiming the pimento at a tablemate.

- You should know without asking that dark meat is below the turkey's waistline and light is above. The mention of turkey "breast" should not cause any titters.

- You should keep your mitts off the paper turkey centerpiece. Do not poke at his accordion tail. Do not make him a hat with a pickle. Do not put a little pile of raisins under his tail.

- Your linen napkin should remain on your lap like a loincloth. It should not be modeled as a head scarf, an arm sling, or a Michael Jackson surgical mask.

- All four chair legs should remain planted securely on the floor at all times.

- You should not suck the middles out of the deviled eggs or stick out your yellowed deviled tongue and pretend to be a lizard.

- It's always fun to get the wishbone, but not at the risk of flattening small cousins or weak old aunts. Anyone who knocks Aunt Vera's glasses into the gravy or shaves the meringue off one of the cream pies will be sentenced to an extra year away from the "big table."

- You should know without asking that the funny-looking utensil sitting beside the roasting pan is a turkey baster, not a giant eyedropper.

- You should know without inspection that stuffing is comprised of various homely nugget-sized brown components.

- You should know without asking or sampling that you will not like mincemeat pie until you're at least 30.

- No yelling "dibs" on anything on the dessert table. No speed-eating to get there, either.

You should know without inspection that stuffing is comprised of various homely nugget-sized brown components.

- Mashed-potato sculpting is creative up to a point, but this isn't an art gallery. You should not display your masterpiece or solicit critiques.

- This is the toughest challenge yet, but if you want to join the "big table," then refrain from saying "gobble, gobble" at the turkey. That's Uncle Herbert's joke. Got it? Stop rolling your eyes and laugh like you mean it.

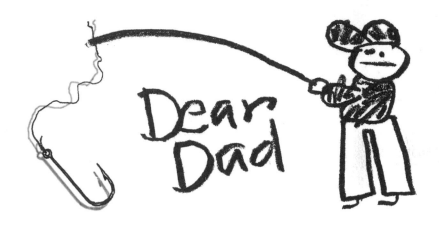

Dear Dad

When You Need a Little Christmas... Now

Becky Freeman

I once cross-stitched a sampler with the well-known saying, "The greatest gift a father can give his children is to love their mother." I might add that the reverse is also true: "The greatest gift a husband can give his wife is to love her children."

One year, our son Gabriel, the day after Thanksgiving asked his dad to bring the Christmas ornaments down from the attic. As fathers tend to do when asked to rummage through high, dark storage places on their day off, Scott brushed off Gabe's question, mumbling something about waiting a week or so. Not long after, I found Gabe quietly crying in a corner.

"What's the problem, Gabe?" I asked.

"Mom," he said earnestly, wiping away a tear. "I just want to see the ornaments. I'll put them away as soon as I look at them. I just want to see some *Christmas* today!"

What's a mother to do? I found Scott as quickly as I could and explained the gravity of the situation—that our son had to have a little Christmas right this very minute. Scott climbed up in the housetop, click, click, click. And down he came bearing gifts—a huge old popcorn can filled with Christmas treasures.

Gabe's lashes were still wet as he beamed up heartfelt gratitude to his father, the hero of the hour. Not to worry about me. It's my joy and privilege to stay behind the scenes in thankless anonymity.

Gabe's lashes were still wet as he beamed up heartfelt gratitude to his father, the hero of the hour.

Gabe's heart so overflowed with gratitude that he went to work right away making Scott's Christmas present. He tore a huge piece of cardboard off an old box and set about drawing a scene of his dad fishing. On the end of the crayon-drawn pole he pasted a real string and a real hook. Then came the inscription.

Dear Dad,
   I love you more than fish love worms. I will never forget this Christmost.
                              Love, Gabe.

I loved seeing my child share open admiration for his daddy—even more than fish love worms.

Shop 'Til You Drop

Karen Scalf Linamen

We've just survived the busiest shopping day of the year.

Of course, I'm using the word "we" loosely, referring to American womankind in general. This is because braving the mall on the day after Thanksgiving ranks somewhere, on my personal list of favorite things to do, between getting a root canal and fishing a toddler's favorite stuffed animal out of the toilet.

I know that some women thrive on mass shopping frenzies, but I'm not one of them. Maybe it's because I usually begin the day thinking I'm one of the sharks and end up feeling more like the bait.

I'm convinced there are spiritual grounds for not going shopping the day after Thanksgiving. After all, isn't there a verse somewhere that promises rest for those who have labored and

are heavy laden? By the time Thanksgiving is over, I've not only labored hard, but I'm feeling pretty heavily laden with all the stuffing and pumpkin pie I've just consumed. I feel like I've earned a rest. I am not inclined to wake up at daybreak on Friday morning with an insatiable desire to haul my tired, bloated body through hordes of crazed holiday shoppers.

Oh sure, once in awhile I find myself feeling seduced by the notion of saving money at all the first big Christmas sales, but I've learned how to resist temptation. My strategy for getting safely through the Nation's Favorite Shopping Day is to put my credit cards and car keys under lock and key—and then swallow the key. This means there's no possible way I can answer the call of the mall until sometime the following morning or after a trip to the emergency room, whichever occurs first.

I realize I'm missing out on some really good sales.

But think of all the money I'm saving on stress therapy.

Of course, Christmas shopping is stressful even without the crowds. This is because it requires finding The Perfect Gift for roughly four dozen family members, intimate friends, business associates, acquaintances and near strangers, not to mention the couple that has been sending fruitcake for years despite the fact that you have no earthly idea where you met them or who they are.

Sometimes I long for a good old-fashioned Walton Christmas. You know, the kind where you give someone an apple or wooden whistle and they go into cardiac arrest from sheer ecstasy.

Sometimes I long for a good old-fashioned Walton Christmas.

Of course, I can't say for certain which is the more difficult task: Finding The Perfect Gift for friends and family... or dropping hints to help my husband shop for me.

One year for our anniversary Larry bought me a nightgown. You're probably thinking, *So far so good...*

He bought it from The Disney Store.

The front of the gown featured a life-sized illustration of Rafiki. (Just in case you don't have children, or you have children but have spent the past five years living on Mars, Rafiki is the wizened old baboon guru in the Disney movie *The Lion King.*)

But perhaps the most intriguing part of the gift was the matching pair of socks that looked like baboon feet.

Now, if the love of your life has never given you a pair of knitted baboon feet, you probably don't know the true meaning of the phrase "Academy Award–winning performance." I'll bet Meryl Streep couldn't have feigned a more convincing performance of ecstatic gratitude, although I think I could have gushed far more convincingly over just about anything else, including an apple or a wooden whistle.

In other words, I tried to appear grateful, but I don't think I did a very good job because Larry figured out right away that I wasn't too crazy about the gift. He's pretty astute about these things. Of course, it's possible that I tipped him off. I think it happened right after I opened the box, right about the moment I blurted, "Ahh . . . I hope you kept the receipt."

Okay, so maybe I'm an ingrate. Apparently I not only keep my eyes peeled for The Perfect Gift when I'm shopping for my friends and family, but I also look for it when unwrapping presents addressed to me.

Maybe I'm looking in the wrong place.

The Bible tells me that "every good and perfect gift comes from above."

Oh, sure, I'll be the first to admit that the Lord has sent a few things into my life that I'd love to return. There are times I take an initial look and blurt, "Ahh, God, I hope you kept the receipt . . . " But hindsight usually shows me that what he gave was exactly what I needed after all. There are even a few gifts that I suspect will require the kind of hindsight I can only get in heaven. Who knows? Those might turn out to be the most perfect gifts of all.

I'm learning to trust the Giver, even when I don't always understand the gifts.

Most of the time, however, the gifts he gives exceed my wildest hopes and dreams.

The fact is that God's gifts—unlike the purchases of harried Christmas shoppers, well-meaning husbands, and other mere mortals—are never the wrong size, color, or pattern.

It'll be interesting to see what gifts he has in store for me this coming year. Although I don't mind admitting that, if I have my druthers, baboon socks won't be anywhere on the list.

2

The Chaos Theory
of Christmas

But Can She Drive a Sleigh?

Shirley Temple

I stopped believing in Santa Claus
when I was six. Mother took me
to see him in a department store
and he asked for my autograph.

Christmas, a Labor of Love

Karen Scalf Linamen

I don't know why Santa gets all the credit.

After all, what family do you know in real life where the man of the house is the driving force responsible for making Christmas happen? I can't think of many. The truth is, we women carry the lion's share of responsibility—and the privilege—of creating memorable holidays for the folks we love.

I think women shoulder the bulk of the work because a successful Christmas requires skills that come more naturally to women than to men.

Like spending massive sums of money.

And that's just for starters. Women are also better at manipulating unwieldy pieces of wrapping paper, as well as

knowing the behind-the-scenes politics of all our friends so that uncomfortable combinations of people don't show up at the same Christmas party. We're also ahead when it comes to remembering the correct spelling of the names of people on our gift list, including distant relatives, bosses, and co-workers, children's teachers, and even our own children. (And I only say this because, several weeks after my daughter Kaitlyn was born, I overhead her dad misspelling her name to a well-wisher on the phone!)

Pulling off the perfect Christmas also requires an under-standing of the nuances of giblet gravy, an ability to whip up an angel costume in twenty minutes or less, and a mastery of the perfect pie crust. (My secret? After I remove the pie crust from the freezer, I make sure I peel off the cellophane and cardboard and label before pouring in the filling.)

Women have these skills. Men don't.

This is why you can't convince me that Mrs. Claus isn't the unsung hero. Don't tell me she's not behind the scenes, coaching her husband every step of the say. I can hear her now, peering over his shoulder as he makes out the gift list: "Santa, honey, don't even THINK about giving that new garage-door remote to newlywed Mrs. Jones. She's going to be much happier with the perfume. Trust me."

I can see her following him to the sled with last-minute shopping instructions: "Target has special holiday hours, so you don't have to rush. There's a sale on Pokémon backpacks at Sears, and whatever you do, DON'T go to Bath World—this is Wednesday and senior citizens get a 10 percent dis-count, so the place will be crowded and you won't be able to maneuver the aisles for the walkers. Did you remember the list? Your wallet? Good. And if I'm not here when you get home, the Scotch tape is in the top left desk drawer, and wrapping paper's in the hall closet."

I can even hear her coaching her husband as he's getting dressed on Christmas Eve: "I don't care if anyone sees you or not. The black dress socks and baseball cap are tacky. Wear something else. And don't try to tell me your red suit is dirty, because I picked it up from the cleaners just this morning."

If you're like me, you take your role as Christmas-maker very seriously. Indeed, Christmas is upon us and right about now you and I are toting lists of about two million last-minute things that need doin' before December 25th. It's not that men and kids don't help with the planning, shopping, cooking, and decorating, but, if women were removed from the picture, Christmas dinners would include tater tots, and two out of three gifts would come from Home Depot.

Christmas depends on us, ladies. The success of the coming holiday is on our shoulders.

Yes, women make Christmas.

It's our labor of love.

Which makes me think of another woman, a woman for whom Christmas was a labor of love in a very real sense of the word.

Because, a long time ago, there was a woman who held Christmas, not on her shoulders, but in her arms. Like you and me, she had the privilege of shaping Christmas, but it wasn't through the labor of her hands. Indeed, Christmas entered the world through the painful rending of her pregnant body, and then she held him in her arms as he slept.

As I'm rushing through the last hectic days before Christmas, it's not a bad time to remember that, as well-intentioned as they may be, my efforts don't "make" Christmas. God did that—through Mary—2,000 years ago. Which makes Christmas complete and perfect, just the way it is.

If I have any goal this December, maybe it should be to celebrate Christmas the way Mary did: by embracing the person called Christ.

Well, that…and staying away from Bath World on Wednesdays.

Lights, Camera... Too Much Action

Jim Killam

Some people, it's said, enjoy a love affair with the camera. My kids just like to make faces at it.

They've reached that tender age group—over 4, under 10—that separates the great photographers from those who quit the business to go work at the slaughterhouse. Kids in this age bracket delight in making the same faces I made at that age, thinking I was the most hilarious kid on Earth. Look at my family albums from those years and you'll see four smiling, happy people and one 9-year-old pushing his cheeks together, guppy style, and looking cross-eyed at the

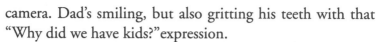

camera. Dad's smiling, but also gritting his teeth with that "Why did we have kids?" expression.

I'm doing a lot of the gritting now, as my three kids make their own cases for being absolutely the most hilarious people on the planet. All the while, I'm thinking, "I paid HOW much for this?"

Not that we ever had an easy photo session, even when the kids were too young to make faces. I think I'm being repaid. One memorable night comes to mind, when my wife had gotten a Sears coupon for a Christmas photo package. Our second son, Zachary, was just four months old and we'd never gotten studio photos of him with older brother, Ben.

Ben, like any firstborn child, was an old pro at this by age 2 ½. But he'd never had a supporting cast. Zack liked to smile but couldn't yet sit up by himself (this becomes important later).

> We reasoned there wouldn't be a line because it was suppertime, only to find a dozen other sets of parents who had reasoned the same thing.

We put the kids in Sunday outfits and tied a huge bib on Zack so he wouldn't slobber all over himself. We arrived at the store about 6 p.m., reasoning there wouldn't be a line because it was suppertime, only to find a dozen other sets of parents who had reasoned the same thing. My wife signed us in, saw six names in front of ours and figured we were looking at about an hour's wait. So we decided to do some shopping in the meantime.

Shopping in a mall with a 2½-year-old is next to impos-

sible (I want this! I don't want to ride in the stroller! Can we go to McDonald's? I filled my pants). Add to that an infant, who's well-behaved but tends to drop his bottle down escalators and spit up on the potted plants, and the Home Shopping Network doesn't seem like such a stupid idea after all.

Anyway, the hour passed (it only seemed like two months), and we returned to the line, where now there were only five names ahead of ours. And that was just on List A, the people having pictures shot. List B, the people picking up their pictures, filled two more pages. My wife took Ben to deal with the aforementioned pants problem. Zack and I found a chair.

The lines stretched beyond the photo department, through Bedroom Furnishings and into Hardware. While kids fidgeted, cried, screamed, played with $200 crystal lamps or tested hacksaws, most parents sat on the hard plastic chairs, staring blankly as if waiting for a firing squad.

Finally, I think it was about midnight, they called our names. We carted the kids into a small studio, Climate Controlled for Your Comfort at 137 degrees. Before long, I'd have gladly traded places with anyone on Death Row outside.

Zack, remember, couldn't sit up by himself, so my wife and I took turns holding on to the back of his sweater, puppet style, our arms hidden by a blanket that would have kept us plenty warm on Admiral Byrd's polar expedition. Ben sat on the other side and did just fine until he got tired of sitting still (about 30 seconds, by my watch).

The challenge was getting them both to smile at once. Over the next 45 minutes, Zack fussed, drooled, cried and or sunk into the blanket. He did finally manage a few smiles.

Ben, who at that age usually was pretty good about smiling when he was supposed to, took on a Clint Eastwood-like leer whenever Zack smiled. Feel lucky, punk?

Meanwhile, a second photographer had been brought in to help. The two of them jumped around, waved their arms, made zoo noises and, when the boys finally smiled at the same time, dropped to the floor on their stomachs and out of the camera's sight while squeezing the shutter. We used to do basically the same exercise in grade-school gym class. So, in case you ever wondered, there is a practical application for squat thrusts.

It took those 45 minutes to take six pictures. The photographers and parents were drenched in sweat. The kids were tired, cranky and hungry. My wife had forgotten the coupon. Just to make myself feel better, I crossed my eyes and made the guppy face at the cashier as we left.

A So-Called Tree and Thee

Charlene Ann Baumbich

7:00 A.M. I can't believe I had anything to do with selecting the fake Christmas tree swallowing up my living room, but it's true; in fact, I was the instigator. Battle scars from previous years had worn me down. Wars that went like this:

"George, I don't care if this fresh green tree costs $40, we only buy one a year."

"I'm not spending forty bucks on a Christmas tree. It won't fit in the living room anyway. What are you gonna do? Cut three feet off the bottom? Why spend forty bucks buying one this big, and then cut it off? No."

"Mom, here's a nice one," Brian says, dragging his giant of a selection toward the pouting me.

"Brian, that won't fit in the living room."

"Fine. I'll keep looking."

George appears with a shrub. Honestly, it's so small it should have been a house plant, and I tell him so. He tosses it aside and disappears around the corner.

Bret falls in love with a couple trees no one likes, although my and his tastes seem to be the closest.

And the war continues, turning our tree-buying adventure into an annual family pain in the poinsettia.

We travel to another lot, where all the trees are $12.95. Finally, all worn down, we get "whatever." The tree ends up being so dry that we're afraid to turn the lights on. Every year I threatened to buy a fake one; every year I hated myself for the suggestion.

But this year, everything changed.

As I sit here in the early morning hours staring at the still-naked tree, sipping my second cup of tea, I wonder what's happened to me. How did I stoop to this: an artificial, man-made piece of seasonal greenery that replaces years of sap-running, fragrant tradition? Even if we do get to avoid the tree-lot blues.

> How did I stoop to this: an artificial, man-made piece of seasonal greenery that replaces years of sap-running, fragrant tradition?

Perhaps the slide began last year when, because of a heavy work load, I ran out of time to bake Christmas cookies. Oh, I managed to crank out one batch of cutter-cookies, but not the usual dozens that once consumed all my Tupperware bowls.

Or maybe it snuck up on me the Christmas before last when my oldest son didn't make it home for the holidays. What was the point of creating my usual plethora of stunning bows only to have to smoosh them into flat wads when I packed them? In fact, there was only time for a few curlicues, since I had to make an extra UPS run to send Bret's packages away, instead of hiding them for Santa's appearance.

So here we are, me and this so-called tree. Setting my teacup on the arm of the couch, I uncurl my legs from under me and deliberately move across the room to reshape a few of the stiff wire branches. Task completed, I kneel at the foot of the 7-1/2 foot imitation thing and scan its depths.

The tree becomes a blur as I mourn for Christmases past: dawn-breaking giggles, carrots left by the fireplace for reindeer, endless hours spent in Santa's line slicking hair into place for photos, cookies decorated with fingerprints, broken ornaments…excitement. Even the days of tree wars.

"So," I say to sleeping Butch, sniffing on my way to the kitchen, "It's a three-cup morning." His eyes roll open and focus on me for a moment. "And I deserve one."

My saturated tea bag looks okay. But the fact is, it can make only weak tea now, tea that just isn't satisfying like the first serving. Tea that fills the cup, but somehow isn't really tea.

I pour the brew down the sink after one sip, seat myself in the chair across from the tree, and invite the dog to climb up into my lap.

The sun has come around a bit, brightening the room, breathing a whisper of life into the meticulously placed branches. I notice for the first time there isn't one needle stuck in the carpet. I won't have to vacuum, I think.

4:00 P.M., with an armful of groceries, I arrive home just as rosy twilight shadows cast their way into my living room, landing on The Tree. We have never brought home such a perfectly shaped tree. Each limb is balanced and looks sturdy enough to showcase the heavy, gold spray-painted, macaroni ornament our son, Brian, had presented to us so many trees ago.

Yes, when we drag our eight boxes of decorations down from the attic tonight, this humongous tree won't have a lick of trouble harboring our years' worth of homemade treasures.

And I won't have to worry about fires.

It's a good year for an open house, I decide. Within five minutes, I pick the date and make a list of hors d'oeuvres. I'll send invitations with our Christmas cards. I'll bake at least two batches of cookies. After all, I'll have time because I won't be vacuuming needles every day. I'll make a bowl of yuletide punch. This will be the year for a new tradition: fresh garland draped around the place. Fragrant. Inviting. Homey.

"I'll get a picture taken with Santa Claus," I chirp to Butch. He groans, as if disapproving. I scratch his head and fantasize about grandchildren.

My husband and son arrive home and grumble about the tree. We talk about Christmas trees past, including many a Charlie Brown tree, hours of arguing over too fat or tall or small or wide or expensive. We laugh a lot.

We pop frozen pizzas into the oven while unraveling our day's happenings; I unfold my new tradition idea. We quickly unpack the boxes labeled "tree decorations" and consider

buying an extra string of lights. The garland idea is a hit, and so is the party.

By evening's end, the tree is spectacular, woven and crammed with pieces of our lives. The halls are decked and sugarplums are doing their warm-ups. It's time to unpack the last box.

Wise men and camels are gently anchored in billows of "angel hair." The Child emerges from the tissue that swaddled him. He gazes at me from the manger.

All is well.

Dear Santa

Debbie Farmer

Dear Santa,

I've been a good mom all year. I've fed, cleaned, and cuddled my two children on demand, visited the doctor's office more than my doctor, sold sixty-two cases of candy bars to raise money to plant a shade tree in the school playground, and figured out how to attach nine patches onto my daughter's Girl Scout sash with staples and a glue gun.

I was hoping you could spread my list out over several Christmases, since I had to write this one with my son's red crayon on the back of a receipt in the laundry room between cycles, and who knows when I'll find any more free time in the next eighteen years.

Here are my Christmas wishes:

I'd like a pair of legs (in any color, except purple, which I already have) that don't ache after a day of chasing kids. I'd like arms that don't flap in the breeze and that are strong enough to carry a screaming toddler out of the candy aisle in the grocery store. I'd also like a waist, since I lost mine somewhere in the seventh month of my last pregnancy.

> I'd also like a waist, since I lost mine somewhere in the seventh month of my last pregnancy.

If you're hauling big ticket items this year, I'd like a car with fingerprint-resistant windows and a radio that only plays adult music, a television that doesn't broadcast any programs with talking animals, and an invisible closet where I can hide and talk on the phone.

On the practical side, I could use a talking daughter doll that says, "Yes, Mommy," to boost my parental confidence, along with one potty-trained toddler, two kids who don't fight, and three pairs of jeans that zip all the way up without the use of power tools. I could also use a recording of monks chanting, "Don't eat in the living room" and "Take your hands off your brother," because my voice seems to be out of my children's hearing range and can only be heard by the dog. And please, don't forget the Play-Doh Travel Pack, the hottest stocking stuffer this year for mothers of preschoolers. It comes in three fluorescent colors guaranteed to crumble on any carpet and make the in-laws' house seem just like home.

If it's too late to find any of these products, I'd settle for

enough time to brush my teeth and comb my hair in the same morning or the luxury of eating food warmer than room temperature and not served in a Styrofoam container.

If you don't mind I could also use a few Christmas miracles to brighten the holiday season. Would it be too much trouble to declare ketchup a vegetable? It would clear my conscience immensely. It would be helpful if you could coerce my children to help around the house without them demanding payment as if they were the bosses of an organized-crime family. Could you please make my toddler not look so cute sneaking downstairs to eat contraband ice cream in his pajamas at midnight?

Well, Santa, the buzzer on the dryer is ringing, and my son saw my feet under the laundry-room door and wants his crayon back. Have a safe trip and remember to leave your wet boots by the chimney and dry off by the fire so you don't catch cold. Help yourself to cookies on the table, but don't eat too many or leave crumbs on the carpet.

Oh, and one more thing Santa: you can cancel all my requests if you can keep my children young enough to believe in you.

Always,
Mom

Merry Christmas (with Cramps)

Jack Hayford

I had a *déjà vu* of sorts a few Christmases ago. I had the opportunity to relive one of my earliest highlights of the season.

My first bicycle was the centerpiece of Christmas 1943. World War II was in full swing, and with all metal resources committed to the material needs of the conflict, new bikes were impossible to come by. But somewhere, my dad had found and fixed up an old one, repainting it in the most stunning red-black combination any kid could want. It was a completely unexpected, now unforgettable moment when I was told, "Close your eyes! Don't peek!" and then was allowed

to open them after the bicycle had been silently wheeled into the living room and placed by the tree.

My second bicycle-for-Christmas was in 1979.

I was equally unprepared for the surprise. But this time it was three weeks before Christmas—and there was good reason for the early delivery.

Anna and the kids had sat me down in the living room with the same admonition: "Close your eyes! Don't peek!" Then I heard the patio door slide open. I knew something was coming in, and I couldn't wait. The kids whispered excitedly while the fire on the hearth chuckled with good cheer.

"Okay, honey," Anna said at last. "You can look now."

I looked. I laughed.
I jumped in the
air like a nine-
year-old.

I looked. I laughed. I jumped in the air like a nine-year-old. The grin that took over my face lasted until my cheek muscles hurt. I hugged Anna and each of the kids. I was *really* excited.

The earlier-than-Christmas arrival of my new bike was timed to allow its availability for the Annual Hayford Father-Daughter-Bike-Outing. Christy, our youngest daughter, was eleven at the time, and our bike-riding junkets were becoming legendary. We rode together all the time, but my bike was old and fading fast. The new one made possible our pursuit of a Christmas dream. Each year, as soon as she was out of school, we set our hearts to really take a ride—to take a *long* one. As she grew older each year, the distances extended. We enjoyed being with each other, and we enjoyed the challenge of being stretched…together.

Now, with my new bike to match hers, we determined to go *fifty* miles. For neighborhood-type bikers, that's no small feat, and we braced for the event with high expectations.

It was a cool December morning when we set out, ready to make biking history in the San Fernando Valley! We pedaled down Hazeltine to Riverside Drive, east to Coldwater Canyon; south (but up hill, and I mean UP HILL) to Mulholland Drive, west, with lots of ups and downs along the southern crest of our Valley's rim, past one beautiful overview after another. We went down Hayvenhurst, west on Ventura Boulevard, and wove a path ending up at the westernmost point—Fallbrook Avenue, in Canoga Park. Wending our way north and east we pedaled along the base of the dam near Rinaldi and Sepulveda, rode under two freeways (this IS Los Angeles)—glided down Laurel Canyon, and ended up home about six hours after we left.

The outing, however, was not without crisis. The year of my new bike—1979—will also be forever marked as the Christmas of "leg cramps to end all leg cramps!"

We had traversed about thirty-five miles of our course when I dismounted to wait for a stoplight where the holiday traffic backed up near Northridge's giant mall.

I'll never forget what happened when I tried to remount. *Agony!*

Sharp, stabbing, gripping, and grinding screams of tissues suddenly lamenting abuse. "You haven't used us like this in twenty-five years!" my muscles seemed to be shouting. I dropped my bike and fell back on the grass at the edge of the curb—groaning and calling Christy to come back to rescue Dad.

She hurried to see what was wrong, looking so alarmed I had

51

to quickly assure her it was only a set of cramps in my calves—not a heart attack! It took a few minutes, but with her help and a brief stint of walking in circles on the lawn near the mall, I regained pedaling capacity and we resumed without further incident. (I did walk with something of a mild limp as I strode to the pulpit the following Sunday . . . to the laughter of the congregation who knew the story already.)

I've often thought of that ambitious Christmas bike ride through the years. Riding those fifty miles with my daughter was a *stretching* experience. But the pain was good, and even the cramps had their place. (I'll always treasure the memory of my eleven-year-old praying so sweetly and fervently for her daddy.) And I also think there's a Christmas message contained in that recollection.

I've concluded that it's good to receive a gift that stretches you. It's good to experience a few cramps in muscles that would otherwise be sedentary.

It's good to be tuckered out rather than stressed out.

It's good to chalk up some adventure with loved ones, breaking old records, pushing out your boundaries, going where you've never gone before.

And with those thoughts in mind, I wish you a Merry Christmas . . . with cramps.

I wish you a Christmas that opens you to gifts of every kind—especially those our loving Father gives in Jesus. And I invite you to be stretched by the possibilities of His gifts.

Yes, really s-t-r-e-t-c-h-e-d.

Don't worry. You'll recover. I did.

Are You Sure the Wise Men Wore Turtlenecks?

Martha Bolton

I remember the year my pastor put me in charge of making the costumes for the Christmas pageant. He and the church board felt I was the perfect person for the job. In other words, I wasn't at the planning meeting.

Now, I'll be the first to admit that sewing has never been one of my talents. The blouse that I made in high school is still on display there showing how not to sew on sleeves. (Evidently there's some unwritten rule about attaching only two.)

But not wanting to disappoint the cast, I agreed to give it my best shot.

I finished the shepherd costumes first, and except for the

Except for the one with the turtleneck and fringe, they turned out rather authentic looking.

one with the turtleneck and fringe, they turned out rather authentic looking.

To my astonishment, I succeeded with the angel costumes as well. A few of them had a little more material than they needed (they could have been an ark cover for Noah), but they worked out fine for the play.

Herod's costume was a cinch, although while pinning it on, I stuck the poor actor so many times he should have been awarded a Purple Heart.

The wise men's robes turned out exceptionally nice also—once I remembered to put in the holes for their heads to go through.

Finally the costumes were sewn, the cast looked terrific, and I couldn't have been prouder as I sat in the audience that night enjoying the pageant just like every other parent—with an instamatic, a Polaroid, and a video camera.

I learned a valuable lesson that evening too. I learned that when the Lord gives us something to do, we should do it. Even when we don't feel qualified for the job, if we'll only trust him, he will make it work out just fine.

As a matter of fact, I've already volunteered to sew the new choir robes for our church. And as soon as the pastor quits changing his phone number, I can get the go-ahead to start.

It's Beginning to Feel a Lot Like Christmas

Karen Scalf Linamen

December is upon us, which means it's that festive time of year when the word "traditions" really means something, when it takes on entire new levels of significance, when merely saying the word conjures a broad spectrum of images and emotions.

Two examples that come immediately to mind are "stress" and "guilt."

Not that stress and guilt can't be festive. They can be. In fact, we probably wouldn't recognize Christmas without them.

Indeed, if we had a completely stress-and-guilt-free Christmas, my guess is that somewhere mid-January we'd find ourselves

asking: "Did we even celebrate Christmas last month? I remember a flawless dinner and beautifully wrapped presents and well-behaved relatives, but for some reason it just didn't FEEL like Christmas. Something was missing, but I can't seem to put my finger on it."

Of course, it's possible that everything would feel more normal as soon as we got our credit-card bill in the mail or discovered those holiday pounds reflected on our bathroom scales. At that point, we'd undoubtedly burst into a rousing rendition of "Jingle Bills" as a result of that new-found Christmas spirit suddenly welling up inside of us.

The weird thing about stress and guilt is that, even though they tend to arrive hand in hand, they come from completely opposite sources. We feel stressed because we're doing too much, and guilty because we think we're somehow not doing enough. You'd think they would somehow cancel each other out, wouldn't you? (Of course, I used to think the same thing about drinking Diet Coke with pepperoni pizza, or adding fat-free ice cream to pecan pie. Oh well. Live and learn!)

Naturally, there are other Christmas traditions besides stress and guilt. Take baking, for example. One of my traditions is to make Christmas cookies from an old family recipe.

My other tradition is to lose the recipe.

To date, my mother has given me the recipe on at least nine different occasions, sometimes more than once for the same holiday.

Another favorite holiday tradition is sending cards. For three years running I kept the tradition of writing a Christmas newsletter, addressing dozens of envelopes to family and friends, and then letting the whole project sit on the

den coffee table until March. Two years ago I finally gave up the dream of sending Christmas greetings to loved ones. Of course, I still experience guilt at not keeping in touch, but at least I can take the time I once spent addressing envelopes and use it for something more constructive. Like calling my mom for that cookie recipe.

In theory, I think traditions are a great idea. After all, there's nothing I'd love better than to lovingly, year after year, craft a Martha Stewart Christmas for my family, complete with beloved traditions that seem to glow with a rich patina bestowed by the passage of time.

In reality, however, traditions are a bit more complicated. They are complicated because they require a lot of planning ("Let me check my calendar")...props ("Has anybody seen the box with the Christmas decorations?")...and cooperation from family members ("What do you mean you have a date with Jason on the night of our Annual Christmas Caroling Extravaganza!?!").

Of course, I'm not saying we shouldn't strive to create meaningful traditions for loved ones.

I'm just saying we shouldn't beat ourselves up when our "Martha Stewart Christmas" turns out more akin to "Holiday Mayhem with Larry, Moe, and Curly."

We shouldn't beat up our friends and family over it, either.

How do we know *when* we're taking this tradition thing

> We shouldn't beat ourselves up when our "Martha Stewart Christmas" turns out more akin to "Holiday Mayhem with Larry, Moe, and Curly."

a little too seriously? I think a big clue for me is when I hear myself bark the following phrases to my kids: "I realize your legs are going numb, but no, you cannot leave the kitchen table. There are still twelve dozen cookies left to decorate, and we're going to sit here and have fun and create a warm memory by decorating every last one of them whether you like it or not!"

You know, there's a great story in the Bible that says a lot to me each December. It's found in the Book of Mark, where Jesus' disciples were criticized for "harvesting" on the Sabbath because they ate a few wheat grains while walking through a field. Jesus responded to the criticism by reminding everyone that "the Sabbath was made for man, and not man for the Sabbath."

Likewise, I try to remind myself that holiday traditions are here to serve me and my loved ones, not the other way around. I never want to compromise peace of mind or harmony in relationships for any given tradition.

Relationships, after all, are more important than ritual.

This is great news. Getting my priorities straight certainly relieves a lot of the pressure I tend to put on myself during the holidays. In fact, in honor of my new commitment to put relationships over ritual, I think I'll call someone I care about for no other reason than to say "Hi" and "I love you." I could call one of my girlfriends…or either of my sisters… or—I know—my mom. I think I'll call my mother.

I needed to call her anyway. I'm going to a Christmas potluck this weekend, and I've been asked to bring the cookies.

See Mother, Funny, Funny Mother!

Author unknown

See Mother. See Mother laugh. Mother is happy.
Mother is happy about Christmas.
Mother has many plans. Mother has many plans for
   Christmas.
Mother is organized. Mother smiles all the time.
Funny, funny Mother.

See Mother. See Mother smile. Mother is happy.
The shopping is all done. See the children watch TV.
Watch children, watch.
See the children change their minds.

See them ask Santa for different toys.
Look. Look. Mother is not smiling. Funny, funny
   Mother.

See Mother. See Mother sew.
Mother will make dresses. Mother will make robes.
Mother will make shirts.
See Mother put the zipper in wrong.
See Mother sew the dress on the wrong side.
See Mother cut the skirt too short.
See Mother put the material away until January.
Look. Look. See Mother take a tranquilizer.
Funny, funny Mother.

See Mother. See Mother buy raisins and nuts.
See Mother buy candied pineapple and powdered
   sugar.
See Mother buy flour and dates and pecans and brown
   sugar and bananas and spices and vanilla.
Look. Look. Mother is mixing everything together.
See the children press out the cookies.
See the flour on their elbows.
See the cookies burn. See the cake fall.
See the children pull taffy. See Mother pull her hair.
See Mother clean the kitchen with the garden hose.
Funny, funny, Mother.

See Mother. See Mother wrap presents. See Mother
   look for the end of the Scotch tape roll.
See Mother bite her fingernails.

See Mother go. See Mother go to the store ten times
  in one hour. Go, Mother, go.
See Mother go faster. Run, Mother, run.
See Mother trim the tree. See Mother have a party. See
Mother make popcorn.
See Mother wash the walls. See Mother scrub the rug.
See Mother tear up the organized plan.
See Mother forget the gift for Uncle Harold. See Mother
  get the hives.
Go, Mother, go. See the faraway look in Mother's eyes.
Mother has become disorganized. Mother has become
  disoriented.
Funny, funny Mother.

It is finally Christmas morning. See the happy family.
See Father smile. Father is happy. Smile, Father, smile.
Father loves fruitcake. Father loves Christmas pudding.
Father loves all his new neckties.
Look. Look. See the happy children. See the children's
  toys.
Santa was very good to the children. The children will
  remember this Christmas.

See Mother. Mother is
slumped in a chair. Mother
is crying uncontrollably.
Mother does not look well.
Mother has ugly dark circles
under her bloodshot eyes.

See Mother
sleep quietly
under heavy
sedation.

Everyone helps Mother to her bed.
See Mother sleep quietly under heavy sedation.
See Mother smile.
Funny, funny Mother.

The Gift of Christmas

Separating the Men from the Toys

Lee Daniel Quinn

Christmas is that time of year when Mother has to separate the men from the toys.

Things Never to Give Your Wife for Christmas

Author Unknown

1. A frying pan, blender, or vacuum.
2. A scale—either for weighing food or her body.
3. Perfume you say you liked when you smelled it on another woman.
4. A copy of the favorite recipe your mother always made you.
5. House shoes like your mother wears.
6. A nightgown one size too small, cut to fit Twiggy, made of polyester, with sleeves that are so tight at the wrists they could pass for tourniquets.

Things Never to Give Your Husband for Christmas

Author Unknown

1. Tickets for two to the opera.
2. Stationery.
3. Cologne you say you liked when you smelled it on another man.
4. Your favorite CD by Barbra Streisand.
5. A book on managing personal finances.
6. A red flannel nightshirt.

Don't Look a Gift Horse in the Slippers

Lynn Bowen Walker

Our first Christmas together, my new beau bought me slippers.

Trying to gauge the future of our relationship based on this one gift, I figured his number one New Year's resolution must be to ditch me. Like escaping the bore you're stuck with at a party by pretending you have to use the bathroom, the slippers must have been his way of letting me down easy.

We've now been married 22 years. Obviously, when it comes to gift-giving, we've had to clear up a bit of confusion.

A week after one recent Christmas, my husband came home from the hardware store and announced brightly, "I got you something."

"You did? What is it?!" I had fantasies of a Chunky candy bar. Or six.

He pulled from a big awkward bag a long handle with what looked like a hedgehog attached to the end. "It's a duster!" he bubbled with pride. "For getting the cobwebs off the ceiling!"

I kissed him on the cheek. "Thank you," I said, "for not giving this to me for Christmas."

He looked bewildered. "You wouldn't have liked it for Christmas?"

"No, I wouldn't."

"Why not?"

"Because it would have sent a message. The wrong message."

The universal Husbands' Creed is "Nothing says love like a dust buster." The Wives' Creed, however, is "Where's the receipt?"

Clear as I am on what I don't want my husband to buy me, I am no expert at buying for him. Every year I buy him a sweater, a t-shirt, and a book on how to be a better fill-in-the-blank.

I do this because I get cold easily, I believe a woman can never have too many fashion options, and I'm intrigued by how-to-improve-your-life-in-five-minutes-or-less, so I figure he must be, too.

Over the years I've also bought him a beer-brewing kit (still unopened), a massaging back rest (conveniently stored in the upstairs closet for easy access, behind the Halloween masks and the spray-on Christmas snow), and a full-length body pillow that, had we kept it, would have meant one of us would have had to go. "That'd probably be a good present if you were dead," he told me.

Choosing gifts for each other is no frolic through the meadow. Lately, when a gift catalog comes in the mail that offers personalized remote-control caddies and other items no man should be without, I casually flip it open, point to my favorite, and ask, "What do you think of this one?"

Choosing gifts for each other is no frolic through the meadow.

"Ugh," he answers.

"Thought so. Merry Christmas, Sweetie." Smooch. "I won't get it for you."

As I said, we've been married 22 years. You can't go that long without learning a thing or two.

What Goes Up Must Come Down

Martha Bolton

I will never forget the Christmas we bought our sons a new swing set. My husband stayed up all night Christmas Eve putting it together. It would have gone faster, but he insisted on doing it the hard way—by reading the "easy to assemble" directions. The directions were about twenty-five pages long, and written in four different languages (none of them English).

The only set of instructions that bore a faint resemblance to our native tongue read as follows: "Insert A into C, bypass B until Step #4, then connect G-1 to D-4, bringing Fig. 8 into alignment with J-7 and overlapping M-3 and P-6. Adjust R-5 to compensate for the 6H4 adjustment."

Since it was too late in the evening to hire an interpreter, my husband tried to decipher the hieroglyphics as best as he could.

He wasn't totally lost, though, because he had *me*. Men *need* their wives close by whenever they're attempting to assemble anything. Who else can answer those tough questions like, "Where's my hammer?" "What'd you do with my screwdriver?" and "Why can't I ever find my tools when I need them?"

Men need their wives close by whenever they're attempting to assemble anything.

After they've worked until the wee hours of the morning to complete the project, who else but a loving wife would have the nerve to point out those three screws and two nuts that are always left over? (No matter what the project, there are always three screws and two nuts left over. Assemble a bike, there are three screws and two nuts left over. Build a doll house, there are three screws and two nuts left over. Personally, I think it's some sort of sick packaging joke.)

In spite of the instructions and the leftover parts, my husband somehow had the swing set up and operational just before dawn broke over the horizon. It was beautiful. A monument to parental perseverance. As soon as the children woke up, we tricked them into going outside. They saw the swing set and were so excited, they stayed out there playing on it for hours.

Now, this story would have remained a warm, wonderful Christmas memory if it weren't for one little fact. That year

we also bought our sons their own tool boxes, each complete with hammer, socket wrench, screwdriver, and more.

While my husband and I were busy making a holiday fire out of all the empty boxes and wrapping paper, the boys had their own little project going. The swing set and tool set together proved to be too much of a temptation, and on one of our trips outside to check on them, we discovered that they had dismantled the entire thing! And they didn't even need directions to do it.

All the pieces were lying in a pile in the middle of the sandbox, and the boys were standing ever so proudly next to them. It was one of those moments when you don't know whether to laugh, cry, applaud their mechanical skills, or return the tool set to the store before they knock out a wall and add a rumpus room to the house.

We opted to laugh about it. Besides, Dad could put it back together again. By now, he was an expert at reading the directions.

"The directions!" my husband screamed, racing to the fireplace just in time to see them swallowed up in flames.

The kids are all grown up now, but Dad still works on it every weekend.

Now let's see…that was *insert A into B…* "

The Gift That Keeps on Giving (Unfortunately)

Dave Meurer

One year I gave my wife what had become an annual Christmas tradition—five more jolly pounds of me. Sadly, Dale's holiday spirit had been declining for several straight years in a row.

"Are you *serious?* You're going on a diet!" she grinched as I stepped off the bathroom scales.

Some women lack an appreciation for Yuletide traditions.

I thus found myself nibbling on thin crackers and swilling down a powdered mix that was supposed to taste like a chocolate shake augmented with "roughage and minerals"

by which the manufacturer apparently meant "sawdust and dirt."

Intellectually, I knew Dale was right about my weight. If I kept up my bad habits I would reach my sixty-fifth birthday weighing as much as the USS *Nimitz* and also facing the very real danger of having military aircraft trying to land on me when I went swimming in the ocean.

I also knew that if I was going to succeed in my quest to slim down, I would need all the moral support I could get, including the assistance of my son Mark, who was just three years old at the time and was *seriously* into Oreos and other epicurean delights that were not now forbidden to me.

"Mark, I have been eating too many goodies, and if I keep it up I might get sick. So, can you help Daddy resist the cookies?"

Mark immediately ran to the kitchen, climbed up on the counter, grabbed an Oreo from the jar, and jumped up and down while squealing, "Neener, neener, neener! You can't have some!"

"Neener, neener, neener! You can't have some!"

This episode did not quite make the grade as one of those "precious moments" that make parenting so rewarding. Don't count on someone making one of those little porcelain statuettes out of the scene.

But with that show of support, I began to diet.

Dale tried to be chipper and upbeat about the ordeal, but even when she put the best china on the table and lit candles for dinner, there was no way she could hide the fact that my plate featured

steamed birch bark and one square centimeter of chicken (skinless and broiled, lest there be any danger of retaining any actual flavor). And the semi-darkness of the candlelight did nothing to hide the scent of lasagna wafting up from Mark's plate.

I stared ruefully at my "dinner" while Dale tried to pretend she was engrossed in studying a map of the United States, but I suspected she was simply trying to hide her plate from me.

"I can't live on this!" I groaned.

"I never knew Ohio had such sharp edges!" Dale exclaimed from behind her map.

I turned to Mark and whispered, "Good news, buddy! As a special reward for being three, Daddy will eat your bread crusts for your tonight!"

"But Mommy says I have to always eat my crust," he said.

"Since when do *you* care what Mommy says?! You NEVER eat your bread crust!" I hissed.

"I like it now," he replied, stuffing it into his mouth.

Fortunately for him, state law at that time forbade selling your preschooler to the circus.

Summoning courage and stamina I didn't know I possessed, I endured immeasurable levels of deprivation and stuck to the diet. It was awful. All I could think about was food. I was literally drooling over the Whopper ads on TV. When I finally climbed back onto the scales, I was shocked to see that I had actually *gained* an ounce. All that suffering and agony for *nothing!* Clearly I was one of those unlucky souls who had a glandular condition that made weight loss virtually impossible.

"It isn't working! I weigh more than I did before I went through all this torture! Oh well, at least we know that there is no point in carrying on with this torment," I said to Dale.

She stared at me coldly with no trace of sympathy.

"You have to be on it for more than forty-five minutes to notice any progress. And don't harbor any hopes that I missed the Snickers wrapper in the glove compartment of your car," she replied.

Vital Marriage Point: Trust is a critical component of any marriage, but this important facet of your relationship will be severely strained if your wife doesn't have enough faith in you to believe that someone else, perhaps a foreign agent, is responsible for the box of Hostess Ho Ho's under your side of the bed.

So I went back to weeks of birch strips and "molecule of chicken breast" as my main staples. And they had all the taste of staples, too, but with less iron.

Call it a revelation, but it finally dawned on me that the calorie spirits have played a cruel joke on everyone who has ever poured skim milk on his morning bowl of unsweetened puffed rice.

As we all learned in high school science class, we live in a closed universe. This means that calories, like energy, cannot escape, they can merely be transformed. Or as a physicist would put it, for every Arnold Schwarzenegger, there is an equal and opposite Danny DeVito. So when someone else plays a game of tennis, some poor slob like me is getting *his* calories.

Imagine the public reaction once this information is widely disseminated.

TV NEWSPERSON: There were several grisly new incidents today of joggers being deliberately run over by enraged women driving Chrysler station wagons. Also in the news, a mob of incensed Weight Watchers descended on Capitol Hill today, demanding enactment of the "Equal Pounds for Equal Height" bill, which was introduced by Congressman Fred "Love Handles" Merkowitz. And over at the U.S. Olympic Training Center, pandemonium ensued when a portly humor writer attempted to force-feed Sugar Babies to members of the U.S. Swim Team.

Having discovered this law of nature, I decided to celebrate the momentous event by indulging in an Oreo.

I was just sneaking my hand into the jar when Mark walked into the kitchen.

"You aren't s'posed to have any!" he exclaimed, eyes the size of baseballs.

"I'm only having one," I explained. "Five or six at the most."

"I'm telling Mom."

"I'll give you twenty dollars," I implored him.

"MOOOOOOOOOOOMMMMMMMMMMMMMMMMMMM!"

I crammed the Oreo into my mouth and began chomping as fast as I could.

Mark burst into tears.

"You aren't *s'posed* to!" he cried.

Uh-oh.

This was suddenly no longer an issue of simply sneaking a cookie. In the eyes of a three-year-old kid, Daddy doing something he knows he should not do, even something as seemingly insignificant as lapsing on a diet, is a mortal failure right up there with violating the Ten Commandments.

"Cum ovfer heer," I mumbled to Mark, and allowed him to watch me as I scraped the mushy cookie out of my mouth and into the kitchen trash can.

I rinsed out my mouth, got down on his level, and let him play "dental inspection."

"I'm sorry, Mark, Daddy gave in to temptation, but I am very sorry. The cookie is *allllll* gone. Is it okay now?"

He smiled, nodded, gave me a hug, and then scampered up the chair and onto the counter and grabbed an Oreo, scraped the filling across his teeth and sang, "Neener, neener, neener! You can't have some!"

If there had been a circus in town that week, this kid would have found himself cleaning out the elephant stalls.

Dale and I continued to make failed attempts at dieting for the next decade plus. But one day, Dale attended a diet workshop that, at its core, taught two simple concepts: (1) eat only when you are actually hungry, and (2) eat only until you are comfortably full.

"This just makes so much sense," Dale said after the first class. "No measuring little cups of this and that, no restrictive menu plans, no more terrible, tasteless food. You just eat when you are truly hungry, and just quit when you are full."

She started losing weight and felt better almost at once.

On the down side, she blew my Danny DeVito theory to smithereens. I was now without excuse. My weight is an issue of self-control, plain and simple.

"Dave, I want to grow old with you. You need to take this seriously," Dale said gently. "The old statement about having 'too much of a good thing' applies to you too."

There is an old hymn that goes, "All to Jesus I Surrender…"

"All" as in "all our excuses."

And all our extra pounds.

I told Dale that next Christmas I plan to give her ten less pounds of me.

"That's the nicest gift you've never given me," she replied. "I can hardly wait to not get it."

Christmas Shenanigans

Robert Hansen

Can't Christmas be done better?

It's a special time, one that I wouldn't want to miss, but there are a few problems involved. I'm not suggesting any changes in the true meaning of Christmas; there's no problem there. I'm speaking about the sheer mechanics of the holiday. There ought to be some solutions for the problems that surround the Christmas season.

The most difficult thing about Christmas is that it is difficult. To kids, this fact is merrily missed because of the joys the day brings. But behind the scenes, parents are working tirelessly in frantic preparations. There's never enough time and never enough days to complete all that must be done.

The perfect solution occurred to me one Christmas and I proposed it to my wife.

"Honey, let's skip all the trappings of Christmas this year. We'll just stick to the true meaning. We'll take all the presents you've slaved over, throw them into large boxes, and store them in the garage. When Christmas comes around next year, we can pull them out again. Think of it. No shopping next year. No wrapping. It'll already be done."

By the look on her face, the first reaction wasn't altogether positive. But I pushed on, confident that the sheer logic of my idea would prevail.

"And the tree, we can put it in cold storage. We'll just leave all the decorations on. That way, the job will already be done for next year."

"The tree won't last that long."

I could tell she was warming to the idea.

"It might still be green. If it isn't, we'll just tell everyone that it's a rare type of Christmas tree—*a brown noble.* Think of all the work it'll save. Next year's Christmas will be a breeze."

I went for a strong closing.

"You work so hard. You deserve a break." I thought I'd presented a compelling case. I looked at her, fully expecting to be covered with praise for my brilliant, timesaving idea.

"You've got to be out of your mind or on something," she retorted.

That wasn't the adulation I expected. Her reluctance was probably due to the fact that one of our children had overheard my suggestion and had a small, tiny, miniscule objection to

> Had my wife forgotten her marriage vows that included a promise to always regard my ideas as brilliant?

the plan. Our son's misgivings seemed insignificant, but without explanation, my wife took his side in the matter. Does loyalty mean nothing these days? Had my wife forgotten her marriage vows that included a promise to always regard my ideas as brilliant?

I wouldn't be deterred by one setback. My mind was already in an improving-the-holiday mode.

Another problem I sought to solve was the lack of surprise at the opening of presents. My childhood memories were of astonishment at the treasures inside those colorfully wrapped packages. Today there's little surprise. Kids are getting all the things they've placed on their list.

To make gift opening more interesting, my wife has tried wrapping small items in oversized boxes. She even tried the rock-in-the-package trick, but today's kids are too smart. They're so adept at shaking and jiggling boxes, that they can usually overcome any attempt at subterfuge. We often hear them declare in delight, "I know what this is." Then they will search our faces for confirmation. Fortunately for me, I rarely know what's in the box (for I lack the proper level of wrapping skills). This proves to be a real advantage as I can honestly shrug my shoulders and offer a blank look.

But the problem remains. I think it's wrong for children to know too much about the contents of the wrapped presents. So, here's my plan.

The presents can be wrapped as usual, except for the labeling that identifies the recipient. Using a code known only to my wife and me, we mislabel every package. As Christmas draws near, we watch with delight as the children try to determine what's in the boxes with the mislabeled name tags. It will be a thrill to see the confusion on their faces. What fun!

When it's time for the present opening, all the packages are distributed. A pile of gifts surrounds each bewildered child. Then, we reveal our clever trick. Each child is instructed to trade places with each other. In this way, we match them with their actual presents. Their distraught faces beam with joy. It's then that they recognize our brilliance and concede that we've won the game, at least for that year.

That would be a moment to treasure and perhaps one to be recorded on videotape. Of course, the same technique will not work again. Thus begins a prolonged battle to keep the contents of the wrapped packages as a surprise. I imagine, a few years down the road, the correct names can be placed on the presents. The children, of course, won't believe it then. Hence, it's another victory.

I'm convinced a little surprise, now and then, is a healthy thing. I know God never lets life get too predictable. Whenever I think I have it all figured out, he inevitably throws me a curveball instead of a fastball. I believe, like my kids, I'd rather get fastballs all the time. But my Father in heaven knows what he's doing. I'm pretty sure this unpredictability has something to do with a thing called "faith"—that terrible and yet wonderful concept we're supposed to learn to live by.

And so, when my wife and I try some of my surprise Christmas techniques on the kids next year, I'll be on solid ground. If they complain, I'll just say that it's a spiritual thing, something I learned from God. How can they argue with that?

Show Me the Money

C. Ellen Watts

While visiting our daughter Andrea and her family at Christmas, we didn't forsake our tradition of holiday stockings for old and young alike. First our son-in-law Larry and then our daughter exclaimed when they found the $50 bills we had tucked in theirs.

When our eight-year-old granddaughter Sara discovered the $5 bill in the toe of her stocking, she couldn't help but compare.

"Oh, dear," she said, "my zero fell off!"

Gifts That Make Mom a Packrat

Martha Bolton

They're in my attic. Boxes and boxes and boxes of them. They're from kindergarten, first grade, and all the way through high school. Tests, term papers, science projects, school-play costumes, priceless works of art—I've kept them all, tucked safely away there. Why? Because that's what moms do. Those yellowing pieces of paper and gallery-worthy crayon drawings are our prized possessions. No, we wouldn't get much for them on eBay, but to us they're more valuable than an original Van Gogh. Why? Because one look and they bring back emotion-filled memories of children whose youthful faces have long since been replaced by adult ones.

These one-of-a-kind treasures take us back to a magical place where giggles, cuddles, and chest-squeezing child hugs once melted our hearts and made all the troubles of our day go away. That plaster-of-Paris hand print presented by a wide-eyed, six-year-old child one Christmas; the macaroni necklace crafted by a four-year-old in Sunday school; the glitter-and-cotton-ball purse an eight-year-old surprised us with one Mother's Day—give up these masterpieces? Would anyone dare ask the Louvre to give up the *Mona Lisa?*

These one-of-a-kind treasures take us back to a magical place where giggles, cuddles, and chest-squeezing child hugs once melted our hearts.

The photo ornament, the hand-painted plate, and any number of other beloved handmade gifts are our tickets for countless journeys back to a place where love, real and un-complicated, is captured and frozen in time. They sit in the attic awaiting each visit. And even though someday we may be too old and weak to keep carting these treasures from house to house, old attic to new attic, we still don't have to let go of them. That's what professional movers are for.

Putting the "X" in X-Mas

Paul M. Hampton

Three weeks before Christopher's fourth Christmas, he was having trouble understanding there was nothing he could do to make it come any sooner. So we came up with a plan.

We circled December 25 on a calendar posted on the refrigerator and each evening, Christopher's job was to mark off another day. Less than a week into this ritual, my wife and I went out while a babysitter watched Christopher.

When we arrived home, our son was fast asleep. But in the kitchen, he certainly had been busy. Every day up to December 25th had been marked with a big black X.

Gifts That Keep on Giving (Me a Headache)

Patsy Clairmont

I do crafts. No, wait, that's not quite right. I own crafts. Yes, that helps to bring into focus the blur of materials stuffed into assorted baskets, drawers, and boxes in my attic and basement.

My craft addiction has left partially done projects pleading for completion. I have snarls of thread once meant to be used in needlepoint and gnarly-looking yarn intended for an afghan. I have how-to-books worn from my reading and rereading of the instructions. (I love reading; it's the doing that bogs me down.) Swatches of material, florist wire, paint brushes, grapevines, and (every crafter's best friend) a glue

gun—along with a myriad of additional stuff—greet me whenever I open my closet.

Every time I'm enticed into purchasing a new project, I think, *This one I'll do for sure.* I've attempted everything from oil painting, floral arranging, quilting, and scherenschnitte (the German art of paper cutting) to quilling.

"Quilling?" you ask. For those of you unfamiliar with it, this craft requires you to wind itsy-bitsy, teeny-weeny strips of paper around the tip of a needle. Once they're wound, you glue the end, using a toothpick as an applicator so your paper coil doesn't spring loose. Then, with a pair of tweezers, you set your coil onto a pattern attached to a foam board, securing it with a straight pin. You are then ready to start the paper-twirling process over again. To be a good quiller, it helps if you, the crafter, are wound loosely. I believe quillers (at least this one) have to be a few twirls short of a full coil to attempt this tedious art.

> I believe quillers (at least this one) have to be a few twirls short of a full coil to attempt this tedious art.

You may be wondering how many of those paper tidbits one needs to finish a piece. That depends on the size of your pattern. I chose a delicate, little snowflake. Taking into consideration that I'm a beginner (which is still true of every craft I've ever tried), I decided to select a small pattern and not overwhelm myself. (This would be like saying, "I think I'll go over Niagara in a barrel rather than a tub in hopes I won't get so wet.")

When I started my snowflake, I thought, *I'm going to make one of these for each of my friends and put them on the outside of their Christmas packages.* After five hours and a minuscule amount of noticeable progress, I reconsidered. *I will give these only to my best friends and include them in their gift boxes.*

A week later, I realized I didn't have a friend worth this kind of effort; only select family members would get these gems. And they would be all they'd get. I thought I would also include a contract for them to sign, agreeing to display their snowflakes well lit, under glass, in a heavy traffic area of their homes, all year.

Fifteen hours into my little winter-wonder project, I decided that this would be the first and last paper wad I'd ever make . . . and I'd keep it for myself. It could be handed down in my family, generation after generation, in a time capsule, after my passing. I often wondered who the flake really was in this venture.

I seem to be more into ownership than completion . . . and then I feel guilty.

Words like *responsibility, follow through,* and *moderation* get lost in the shuffle as I push back one box of crafts to move in my newest project.

What happened to the notion "Waste not, want not"?

That's a great line. I wonder how it would look in cross-stitch? Oops, there I go again.

Some Assembly Required (and a Little Prozac Wouldn't Hurt Either)

Martha Bolton

I remember the Christmas my husband and I bought a new bicycle for one of our boys. Our son was thrilled, excited, elated. But then, right in the midst of all the merriment, something happened to ruin the moment. He asked us to put it together.

I tried to get him just to play with the parts for a month or so, but he wasn't interested. I ripped the picture of the bike off the carton and told him to straddle that for a while. He merely shook his head. He wanted the bike itself, the real

thing. And he wanted it to look exactly like the photo.

So, my husband grabbed his toolbox, I grabbed some aspirin, and we began. We labored. We sweated. We worked into the night. Finally, we got the box open. Then came the real fun—that of trying to decipher the instructions that were written in a hardback trilogy and had more steps than the Taj Mahal.

They did promise, though, that the only tools we would need would be a screwdriver, a hammer, and an adjustable wrench. But, by the time we were done, we had used every tool in the garage *except* the screwdriver, hammer, and adjustable wrench. (Although, at times, several uses for the hammer did cross our minds.)

After six hours of trying to get A into B, connect D to F, slide G through H while bypassing E altogether until Step #9 (at which point we were to overlap H with I), we finally completed our project. The handlebars were on sideways, the kickstand kicked back, and there were six screws unaccounted for, but we were done.

The handlebars were on sideways, the kickstand kicked back.

"But it doesn't look anything like the picture," my son moaned.

"Sure, it does," I assured him. Then, snatching the picture from his hands, I cut it into tiny pieces, scrambled them to match up with the contraption we had just built, and smiled confidently. "See, now it looks *exactly* like the picture."

"Maybe we should take it back to the store and get some help," my son said. "You know, from the people who made the bike in the first place. They'll know how to put it together."

I had to agree. I'm sure the guy who designed the bike didn't mean for both wheels to be on the same side or the seat to be pointing heavenward.

So we took the bike back to the store and, within minutes, they had it looking and operating precisely as it was meant to. It was beautiful. Our son was thrilled, and my husband and I were in awe of how simple a task it was for someone who knew what he was doing. After all, who better to put a bike together than its maker?

Sometimes we may need a little help assembling our lives, too. No matter how hard we try, we just can't seem to make A fit into B. We work at it and work at it, but it doesn't end up looking anything like it was supposed to. That's when it's time to gather up all the pieces and take them to the Lord. After all, who better to put a life together than its maker?

Gift-Giving Misgivings

Tim Wildmon

Gift giving is great, isn't it? The Bible says it is better to give than to receive. Most of us do get a special feeling when we give someone a gift we know they will love. Birthdays, special occasions, and especially Christmas, are days Americans love to give gifts to one another. And we love receiving them as well.

But did you know that according to a survey by the American Express Travel Related Services Company, one in four of us has actually passed on a gift given to us to someone else? It's true. The American Express Travel Related Services people wouldn't lie about something as important as this!

All I have to say is, for shame! You people kill me! I would never, ever. . . Okay, okay, my hand's up too. But it's been a while. Last Christmas, I think it was.

If gift giving is a great American tradition, I guess passing on a gift someone gave us is a great American tradition as well. Now keep in mind this one-in-four number represents people who actually admitted to doing this. And this is one of those questions that even the people who answer "yes," and are honest, still tuck their heads when admitting to it.

Let's see, it's an ugly sweater your aunt gave you and so you—being the thoughtful type—decide to give it to your brother next Christmas. But what if your aunt who gave you the ugly sweater is there when he opens the box? What then? Answer: tell her you loved the sweater so much that you went out and bought your brother one just like it.

Yes, technically you are lying. Technically.

Now if she starts looking at the tag real close and sees you got the sweater last year for the same discounted price she got it for, and at the same store, then you've got problems.

"Why, if it ain't the same price and store, Aunt Josie, I'll be John Brown. What are the chances of that happening?"

How about that Christmas fruitcake? We've got one in our family that's been passed around for seven years now. Everybody knows it, but no one says anything. It's been in my freezer twice for one year each time. That fruitcake's been in four different states and three time zones. I thought about throwing it away, but I want to see who the brave soul is that actually eats it. Besides, it's kind of a Christmas tradition now.

What are those green things anyway? Are they from the fruit family? I don't think so. I've been to the grocery store many times in my life and not once have I seen those green things among the other fruits such as bananas, apples, and oranges. I've only seen them in fruitcakes at Christmastime, which leads me to believe they aren't fruit at all but are actually unused automotive parts melted down and mixed in with cake mix in hopes that no one will notice. Well, I did. And I, for one, have a rule against eating melted-down automotive parts. And if I'm the only one who believes this, then so be it.

Now we know, again, thanks to the fine folks at the American Express Travel Related Services who wouldn't lie about such things, that 25 percent of us pass on gifts we don't want to others as gifts. But how about the flip side of that? You know, buying some member of your immediate family a gift they have no practical use for, just so that you can use it.

I've got a confession to make here. When I was nine, I did this. Mom gave me a few dollars to buy my little one-year-old brother, Mark, a gift. So I bought him an electric football game. Man, I had a ball with that thing. I wore it out before he was old enough to use it, though. I did let him bang on it a few times just to ease my conscience, and I pretended it was a wet field when he would drool. Sorry, I have to break this to you in a book, bro. Hey, I was told it was the thought that counts anyway.

Speaking of thoughts that count, it was our Heavenly Father who was thinking of you and me when He gave us the

greatest gift of all, His Son Jesus Christ. The Bible says in the gospel of John 3:16, that, "God so loved the world that He gave His only begotten Son, that whoever believes in Him should not perish but have everlasting life" (NKJV).

If we only receive God's free gift of Jesus into our hearts, the Bible promises we will live forever. Simply put, that means when we die we go to heaven to be with Jesus and all those who've gone before us who also trusted in Him.

And the wonderful thing about the gift of Jesus is that we can, indeed, pass it on to others while maintaining His presence for ourselves. In fact, that's what God wants us to do.

And for what it's worth, there are no green things.

Peas on Earth... and Other
Tasty Holiday Tidbits

Good Stuff(ing)

Anonymous

A three-year-old gave this reaction
to her Christmas dinner:
"I don't like the turkey, but
I like the bread he ate."

All Fired Up for the Ladies' Christmas Coffee

Becky Freeman

News travels fast in our small town, and when word got out that I had co-authored a book about worms—*Worms in My Tea*—my status immediately grew. As a matter of fact, I found myself proudly introduced in public places as "the author with Worms." Another friend came up with a promotion ploy—suggesting Mother (my co-author) and I wear buttons that read "Ask us about our Worms."

With that sort of interest, of course, invitations to speak began to pour in. Well, perhaps *trickle* might be a more accurate word for it. (Okay, so I dropped a hint over the phone to the Ladies' Committee Chairwoman from my church that

I just might be available to speak at our annual Ladies' Class Christmas Coffee.)

When I arrived at the home where the coffee was to take place, it looked like it belonged to Martha Stewart on one of her better Christmases. Elegant it was, with a roaring fire in the huge stone fireplace, luxurious furniture covered in rich tapestries, and the entire house accented with holly, ivy, lace, candles, flowers—the works.

By a great miracle I had arrived early, and I soon saw that the hostesses were having trouble with the spout of the gorgeous silver coffee urn. It would not stop dripping. There it stood in the middle of the white damask cloth, nicely lit by a votive candle on either side, its spout creating a puddle in a hastily placed crystal punch cup. I couldn't help thinking that perhaps the Spirit had prompted me to arrive early because He had foreseen my skills would be needed. (Readers of *Worms in My Tea* will already know that I have become somewhat of an expert on leaking things—appliances, car radiators, commodes, sewers. Why wouldn't these skills transfer to an elegant silver coffee urn?)

I jiggled the spout in a more professional manner than the hostess had been jiggling it, and when the puddle continued to grow, I bent low and tried to peer up the spout itself. Clearly I was onto something. A most peculiar odor became apparent—it was followed by a puff of smoke wafting before my eyes. Suddenly the hostesses sprang at me from all directions, beating me about the head and shoulders with towels and tossing cups of water in my general direction. When I realized I had managed to ignite my own hair with the votive candles beside the urn, I did exactly what I had taught my first-graders to do in our "Safety First" course: I stopped, dropped, and rolled all the way to an easy chair where the hostesses insisted I stay until it was time for me to speak.

Suddenly the hostesses sprang at me from all directions, beating me about the head and shoulders with towels and tossing cups of water in my general direction.

"We don't want anything else to happen, Becky," they assured me. I was touched by their concern.

My topic for the morning was, "Taking Time to Wonder as You Wander Through the Season," and I'm sure the ladies were indeed wondering why the hostess had included fragrance of singed hair in the potpourri on her tables. (Considering the elegance of the rest of her decorations, I expect we may have seen the evolution of an entirely new Christmas fragrance, I watch for it every year. It transports one almost immediately to a stable.)

I had planned to end my talk with a moving quote about the love of a father for his young son. At this tender, emotion-charged moment, the Sterno heater on the buffet table suddenly ignited, shooting flames about two feet into the air. It created quite a stir, but our Christmas Coffee Women's Volunteer Fire Department leaped into action, beating the flames with dish towels, trying to subdue the inferno with crystal cups full of punch and coffee, and finally extinguishing the persistent flames with an inverted fondue pot.

When the hostesses looked in my direction, I was thankful

I had been standing at least three yards from the table during the entire event.

Afterward I went straight home, called my mother, gave her all the details of my first speech, and told her how we might need to bring portable fire extinguishers to any future events we might do together. She laughed, I laughed, and then in the background, I could hear my father asking for details. "So, how'd Becky do?"

Though her voice was a bit muffled, I could hear her praise me as only a truly creative mother can: "Honey, she was on fire. The audience simply melted in her hair…uh…I mean *hands.*"

A Turkey of a Dinner

Jana Kaumeyer

In an attempt to develop better eating habits, our family began eating "turkey franks," "turkey ham," "turkey bacon,"
and "turkey burgers." When Thanksgiving came, I made a
beautiful traditional dinner with all the trimmings. But only
after my husband started to carve the bird did I realize how
health-conscious we had become when ten-year-old Katy
asked, "Mom, is this real turkey or 'turkey turkey'?"

Where's the Fire?

Martha Bolton

One of our family traditions is to go out to eat at a nice restaurant every Christmas Eve. After all the shopping, all the wrapping, all the hustle bustle of the crowds, it's a treat to sit down and enjoy an evening of fine dining.

One year we decided to try a new restaurant that had just opened in town. We had heard a lot of good reports, and wanted to check it out for ourselves.

Upon our arrival the maitre d' welcomed us, led us to our table, and proceeded to describe the specialties of the house. One such specialty intrigued my husband—a choice of chicken, shrimp, or beef that we'd cook ourselves on a heated stone at our table.

"Why don't we try it?" he coaxed. "Sounds fun."

"You take me out to a nice restaurant, and I *still* have to cook?" I whined.

"It's all right, honey," he said. "It'll be supervised. Besides, restaurants always keep fire extinguishers on hand."

The kids cast their votes in Dad's favor, and it was now a closed matter. We were going to be cooking our own dinners, and paying $15.95 apiece for the pleasure.

It wasn't long before the waiter brought out our heated stone and placed it in the middle of our table. Setting the tray of meat beside it, he smiled and said, "Enjoy!" before disappearing into the kitchen.

Since it was his idea, my husband was the first to place his chicken on the stone tablet.

"Shouldn't it be sizzling?" I asked, after five minutes of watching nothing much happen.

"Maybe it's cooking internally," he reasoned. "You know, like a microwave."

We threw on some shrimp just to see how they would fare. They, too, sat there.

"Are you sure the tablet's hot enough?" I asked.

He carefully put his finger on the stone. Then two fingers. Then his whole hand, which didn't sizzle any more than the chicken had. We asked for a different stone, but it wasn't much better. At the rate we were going, the meat was going to spoil before it cooked.

When it became obvious that the only thing getting hot was my husband's collar, we decided to review our options.

"We could ask for a third stone," I said, grilling a slice of beef over our centerpiece candle.

"We could change our order," the boys suggested.

"We could go somewhere else to eat," was my husband's recommendation, and once again it received the most votes.

We paid our bill, had the valet bring up our car, and drove to another restaurant about two blocks away. We could smell the aroma of sizzling beef as we pulled into their driveway. They didn't have valet parking, and we weren't going to be eating by candlelight. But they *did* cook our meat for us. And anyway, that glow from their gold arches gave the evening a certain festive feeling after all.

Baking Cookies? Bah! Humbug!

Tina Krause

"This year, no cookie baking!" my eighty-year-old mom chided as we discussed holiday plans. I agreed.

Last year my daughter-in-law Robin decided to host a Christmas cookie-baking day. "Wouldn't it be fun for all the women in our family to get together to bake cookies?" she asked eagerly.

For Robin, Christmas conjures old-fashioned Norman Rockwell scenes of crackling fires, steamy mugs of hot chocolate, and the scent of homemade cookies and holiday breads wafting through the house. Gathered around an old upright piano, family members lift their steamy mugs and

mismatched voices in song. Void of chaos, dirty dishes, and crumpled wrapping paper, the cozy scenes are stress-free and serene.

I looked forward to an entire day of mixing, baking, and decorating about as much as I welcomed a fly in my cookie mix.

My Christmas images differ slightly. Having hosted more events than Martha Stewart and juggled enough pots and pans to make Julia Child look like a kitchen klutz, I looked forward to an entire day of mixing, baking, and decorating about as much as I welcomed a fly in my cookie mix. But in an attempt not to squelch Robin's youthful enthusiasm and holiday spirit, Mom and I agreed.

As the day approached, Robin's excitement escalated. Preparing for the event, she made lists of things we would need to bring. "Oh, by the way," she added, "I don't have a rolling pin. Could you bring yours? And would you mind bringing some extra mixing bowls and measuring spoons? And do you already have sprinkles? If not, I'll buy some more...." Each day she added more items to her list as the phone rang with her requests.

Finally the day arrived. When I picked up Mom, it took all of half an hour to load her bags of bakery gadgets into my car. Seems Mom received a few phone calls, too. Shifting boxes and bags to make room, I squeezed Mom's stuff in with mine.

When we arrived at Robin's, she greeted us at the door with smiles and holiday cheer. "Can I help you bring things in?" she asked warmly as Mom and I trudged to and from the car, handing her bag after bag. Soon my other daughter-in-law, Theresa, arrived, hauling in her carload of bakery items, too. Much like our hostess, Theresa couldn't wait to begin our bake-til-you-break extravaganza.

Only one problem: Mom and I were already ready to break. But like busy holiday elves, we emptied bags, sorted, and set up our workstations while the festive strains of "Joy to the World" played in the background.

After hours of rolling, sifting, sprinkling, and stirring, the "older" ladies slowed down and ambled to the living room for some Christmas carols minus the mayhem. Meanwhile the youthful duo laughed and whirled around the kitchen like two pixies on a sugar surge.

"I'm exhausted," I said as I eased into a chair.

"I am, too," Mom replied, resting her head against the back of the couch. "You know, I just can't keep up like I used to."

Suddenly, the girls noticed our disappearance. "Hey, where'd you guys go?" Robin yelled through the house.

"Yeah," Theresa echoed. "Why'd you stop baking?"

I shifted into my philosophical mode. Why'd we stop baking? Might it have anything to do with the fact that for thirty-plus years on my part and more than a half century for Mom, we have baked and cooked until our wooden spoons squared off at the end and our white rubber spatulas turned yellow? Could it be that Christmas carols and warm fuzzy scenes lose their glow in a cloud of white flour and confectioner's sugar?

"Bah! Humbug! To the baking scene," I mumbled under my breath. But I kept my voice low, like a subdued Scrooge.

"We're coming," I assured the girls with a sigh as Mom and I lifted our sagging bodies with simultaneous groans.

At the end of the day, I determined to simplify the holiday process in the future and concentrate on the real meaning of the season—the coming of Jesus Christ to this earth to redeem us from our sins.

However, I am relieved the younger set has the energy and enthusiasm for the blessed holiday season. And I must admit, a symphony of Christmas carols intermingled with the aroma of hot-out-of-the-oven cookies is warm and inviting—as long as I am eating, not baking them. By the way, Mom just seconded that.

'Tis the Season

G. Ron Darbee

"Dad! Dad!" my son yelled as he burst into the den, interrupting the solitude of my quiet time.

"What is it, and how much will it cost?" I asked, assuming his urgency was financially motivated.

"Nothing, Dad. It's not always about money, you know."

"Sorry, Son. What's so important?"

"You know that father/son bonding stuff you're always talking about? Well, Mom is going nuts, and now would be a great time."

"What did you do?" I asked, concerned that his sudden desire to bond with the old man might somehow stem from a bent for self-preservation.

"Nothing! I mean it."

"Then what did I do?" (It never hurts to check.)

"I don't think you did anything, either," he said. "It's Mom. She was baking Christmas cookies and just started acting crazy. Now she's crying because she can't get the top off the Midol bottle."

"Ohhhh," I said, the situation suddenly clear. "We have what is called a crisis situation, my boy. Conditions require that we make ourselves scarce."

> "We have what is called a crisis situation, my boy. Conditions require that we make ourselves scarce."

"What about Melissa?" he asked, referring to his little sister.

"She's down the block playing with Sarah," I said. "And besides, they never go after one of their own. It's you and me I'm worried about. Where is your mother now?"

"In the garage. She's tearing up your workbench looking for that 'cutting thing.' I think she means the scroll saw."

A chill ran up my spine at the mention of my power tools. "Honey, wait!" I yelled through the walls. "Don't plug anything in. I'll be right there." I turned to my son to relay the game plan. "OK. I'm going in. If you don't hear from me in ten minutes, come and get me."

"No way."

"Chicken," I said, going for the soft underbelly of adolescent pride. "And after all the tight spots I've pulled you out of."

"Don't think I don't appreciate it, Dad. Good luck getting the cap off that bottle." He patted me on the back and sent me on my way.

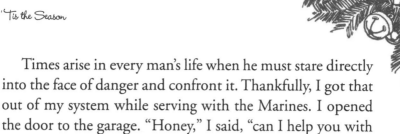

Times arise in every man's life when he must stare directly into the face of danger and confront it. Thankfully, I got that out of my system while serving with the Marines. I opened the door to the garage. "Honey," I said, "can I help you with anything?"

"You can try to take the top off this bottle, or show me how to start the chain saw," Sue said.

Following the manufacturer's instructions, I pushed down while turning and presented my wife with the open bottle. I chose not to flaunt my success at that particular moment and exited posthaste.

Moments later, I returned to the den and found my son deeply engrossed in a game of Nintendo. "Mission completed," I informed him. I pointed to the television screen. "I can tell you were worried about me."

"I knew you could handle it, Dad." He put the game on pause. "Hey, Dad? Why is it Mom always gets like this around the holidays? She really seems to freak out around Christmas."

"Tradition," I said.

"Tradition?"

"Yeah, you know: stringing popcorn and cranberries, carols around the tree, anxiety attack—happens every year. Your grandmother used to get spun up, and her mother before her. It's tradition."

"How come?"

"Mom works hard to make sure everything is just right at Christmas, Ron," I said. "If she gets a little anxious, we can give her some room."

"I know, but you guys are always saying that all that stuff

doesn't matter. Jesus is supposed to be the focus, right? Why does Mom get so worried about the details?"

"I guess she wants everything to be perfect," I said. "You and I both know she understands the real meaning of Christmas. In her own way, Mom is performing an act of service. By sweating all the details, I think she figures it'll be easier for the rest of us to celebrate and enjoy Christ's presence."

"So what do we do?" he asked.

"Nothing," I said. "We sit here and hide in the den like real men."

Grabbing the other controller, I sat on the floor and joined him in his game: Mario and Luigi attempting to avoid the mighty Koopa. One couldn't help but notice the irony.

An hour or so passed and things were looking up for Mario and Luigi. We quit our game and listened for sounds of life outside our sanctuary. All was quiet, no sign of life, save the smell of freshly baked cookies. It was too much for my son, as weak-willed as most boys when matters of the stomach are involved.

"Dad, do you smell those cookies?" he asked, his eyes as big as saucers, a hint of saliva at the edge of his lips.

"No, I do not," I said, squeezing my nose between thumb and index finger. "If you know what's good for you, you don't smell them either."

"Come on, Dad. I can be in and out of there before anyone knows it. I'll just grab a couple."

"I want to go on record as saying this is a mistake," I lectured. "But if you are determined to follow this course of action, so be it. Don't forget the milk."

Following at a distance, I monitored his progress. My boy

edged his way out of the den, through the hallway, and into the kitchen. Deep down, I was rooting for him, though I doubted the probability of a triumphant return. For a moment, it appeared he might succeed.

"Get your hands away from those cookies!" screeched a familiar feminine voice. "Don't you even think about eating them. Those are for Christmas." Ron made a hasty retreat back to the safety of the den.

"You forgot the milk."

"Sorry, Dad. I don't know how it slipped my mind. So what do we do now?" he asked, looking to his mentor for direction. "The cookies are out of the question, and I don't think we want to push Mom right now."

"We could wrap presents," I suggested. "Just the two of us. It might be kind of nice."

"I haven't done any shopping yet, Dad. We've still got a week."

"Yeah, me either. Well, we could go outside and hang the lights. That'll kill an hour."

"You're not going to put the lights up with a staple gun again this year, are you?" he asked. "I'd hate to think electrocution is going to be another family tradition."

"No, I bought these little hooks that were made for the job," I said. "You go bring the ladder out front and I'll pull the lights down from the attic. Oh, and son, have a cookie. I palmed a couple while your mother was yelling at you. Merry Christmas."

"Thanks, Dad. Merry Christmas to you, too."

Holiday Memories

Dale Hanson Bourke

A friend of mine and I were discussing the importance of holiday traditions recently. Both new to the art of mothering, we were suddenly feeling the pressure to establish traditions for our families, "before it was too late." After all, we both had young sons who, we were told, needed meaningful holidays as much as they needed play groups, snug-fitting diapers, and educational toys. Who knew what would happen to our toddlers if we didn't provide the right environment? Would they be ostracized in grade school? Would they grow up and confess to psychological abuse in their formative years?

As the holidays approached, I began taking this task quite seriously—reading books, studying expert advice, listening to

"successful" mothers—when it suddenly occurred to me that my own holidays had been nearly traditionless.

We were suddenly feeling the pressure to establish traditions for our families "before it was too late."

To say my family *always* did things one way would be to deny the essentially spontaneous nature of the Hansons. We never let one celebration serve as precedent for the next. We rarely followed a path we'd walked before. In fact, my memories of holidays are a crazy quilt of sights, sounds, and activities—few tied to one another.

There was the Thanksgiving that we were in the middle of moving and my mother served a turkey roll in the center of her large, handpainted platter. Sitting among the boxes, we laughed until we cried at the sight of the pitiful little processed bird. And there was the year we had our Thanksgiving lunch at a hot dog stand so that we could travel to both grandparents' houses in one day and keep peace among the relatives.

There was the Christmas that my parents let me open "just one gift" on Christmas Eve. Knowing my essentially greedy nature, they counted on my choosing the largest box, which they had filled with nuts. Although we had a good laugh, they sensed my disappointment, and let me open the rest of my presents that night.

And then there was the Christmas morning that the presents arrived in the shower stall. We had no fireplace, so my father explained, with an almost straight face, that Santa

must have lost weight and squeezed through the faucet to deliver the gifts.

I suppose, after reviewing my memories, that there was *one* holiday tradition in my family. The tradition was humor, and it had a way of wrapping itself around all the diverse activities of holidays and other times of the year. It got us through turkey rolls and hot dogs, unexpected presents, and houses without fireplaces. It made our Christmas tree sparkle and gave us moments of joy when we least expected them.

It salved the wounds of childhood, too, and eased me through skinned knees, the deaths of pets, and the disappointments of friendships. It put sibling rivalries in perspective and gave me confidence that I belonged.

If there was one thing we were always able to do, it was to laugh at ourselves and even at each other. Sometimes one of us took it personally and had to be lovingly teased back into the fold, but mostly we all knew that no matter what, we were part of one crazy, loving family. Even if we celebrated holidays erratically or treated tradition irreverently, we still knew that family times were special.

So as I prepare my own young family for the holidays, I'm becoming more relaxed about establishing traditions. My son can probably enjoy the holidays without a special menu, a keepsake ornament, or a carefully trimmed tree. But I don't think he can truly appreciate any holiday without love and humor.

Is the Turkey Burned Yet?

Martha Bolton

Each Thanksgiving families gather around the table to partake of that traditional bird, the turkey.

Now, preparing a turkey isn't as easy as it may seem. You need skill, you need patience, and if you're like me, you need the telephone number of a pizzeria that delivers...just in case.

It's been said that the only difference between a turkey and a Cornish hen is 10 hours in my oven, and I suppose that's true. You see, I don't think I've ever cooked a turkey right. Either it's underdone—meaning when I take it out of the oven, it gets up and walks to the table. Or, it's over-done—meaning my smoke alarm starts playing "Come and Dine."

More often than not, it's the latter problem that I have to deal with. I can take a plump, juicy young tom and turn it into turkey jerky in no time.

I can't exactly pinpoint what it is about turkey that makes it so difficult for me to prepare, but I've never been able to get the hang of it.

Last year, someone suggested I try lowering my oven temperature (I believe it was the fire department). I tried their tip. The turkey took two-and-a-half days to cook. I didn't mind, but my dinner guest hadn't really planned on a slumber party.

The year before that, my mother recommended I cook my turkey in a brown paper bag. I gave that a try, but unfortunately, the paper bag ended up tasting better than the turkey. As a matter of fact, it was the only item anyone took seconds on.

Wrapping my turkey in aluminum foil probably works best for me. It doesn't keep my bird from burning, but at least I don't have to look at it.

This year, though, I think I might try cooking the fowl in one of those plastic cooking bags. That way if it doesn't turn out edible, at least it'll already be bagged for the trash.

But I've decided it doesn't matter how my turkey turns out—whether it's so good everyone raves over it, or so bad my dog runs away until all the leftovers are gone. The important thing is what it represents. Thanksgiving is a day to count blessings, not culinary casualties. And I do have so much to be thankful for: family, friends, health, work, clothing, a home—and especially that little pizzeria down the street that stays open on holidays.

The Call of the Popcorn

Becky Freeman

Last Thanksgiving, our family decided to meet at a lake in Kentucky, one day's drive for each of us. My brother David and his wife, Barb, brought their three-year-old Tyler from Indiana. Tyler met Grannie and Daddy George at the door, his enormous brown eyes wide with excitement as he spied the mammoth bucket of flavored popcorn his grandparents were hauling up the steps.

Imagine Tyler's disappointment when he discovered only a few kernels left in the container. There is no such thing as sinless perfection and sometimes, Mother and Daddy descend into gluttony. Seeing our reproachful eyes, Mother tried to explain.

"How can I tell you that you cannot trust two sensible,

people with ten gallons of popcorn on a long trip in a small car?"

We allowed her time to put away her coat and get a cup of coffee before we began interrogating. Her defense was inspired.

"We hadn't been on the road two hours before I began struggling with visions of caramel-flavored popcorn. I reached into the back where the can occupied half the seat and grabbed a handful to share with Daddy George.

"Before long, we were filling the lid of the can one load at a time, our hands moving from lid to mouth with increasing speed. Soon the rate of speed was such that our hands could not be seen—similar to the blades of a helicopter in flight; two rotors are in motion, but only a blur is visible." (By this time our four children and Tyler were open mouthed, and Mother warmed to her story.)

"Finally, with so many trips to the back seat for refills, the car started to wobble on the highway. My accomplice suggested I try to get the entire can on the front seat with us, but I was not willing to hang out the door in order to accommodate the can. When he suggested I do so, I knew we had to get control of ourselves." She paused dramatically and gazed at the kids.

The popcorn, acting like a million tiny sponges, swelled up until only one of us could ride in the car.

"I reminded Daddy George of you dear children. Our rotor blades slowed and again became hands as they finally sputtered to a belching halt. But then, we made a terrible mistake." She paused for effect.

"We were thirsty and stopped for a tall glass of water. The popcorn, acting like a million tiny sponges, swelled up until only one of us could ride in the car. Daddy George had to tie me on top of the car for the rest of the trip!"

The kids loved it, but Zach and Zeke, so close to being worldly-wise, groaned a lot. "Awww, Grannie..." We may not have been able to transport a turkey to Kentucky for our Thanksgiving table, but there was plenty of ham to go around, thanks to Grannie.

When Is a Leg Like an Ear?

Mary Wanda Little

As our family was enjoying a delicious Thanksgiving dinner, my four-year-old granddaughter stopped chomping on her drumstick long enough to look at her mother, smile, and say, "I really like turkey on the cob."

Let There Be Peas on Earth

Laura Jensen Walker

My husband, Michael, is very big on tradition.

He likes to eat the same foods he grew up with on Thanksgiving or Christmas.

So do I—although I'm willing to be a little more adventuresome now and then and add something new to the holiday table.

Not Michael.

At Thanksgiving he's gotta have his turkey, stuffing, mashed potatoes and gravy, pumpkin pie, yams, corn, and creamed peas.

Well, I detest peas—in any way, shape, or form. And there was certainly no way I was going to cream them—yuck!

However, when my sister, Lisa —who doesn't like to cook—heard that Michael just loved creamed peas, she offered to make them as her Thanksgiving contribution.

When my sister, Lisa—who doesn't like to cook—heard that Michael just loved creamed peas, she offered to make them as her Thanksgiving contribution.

But she told me not to say anything to him because she wanted it to be a surprise.

Now Lisa had never made creamed peas before in her life.

Nor had I, and neither of us had a clue as to how to prepare them.

So she looked in cookbook after cookbook before she finally found a recipe.

Turkey Day arrived, and everyone brought their Thanksgiving specialties to our kitchen. Lisa was one of the last to arrive and she came in bearing a clear glass bowl covered in plastic wrap which she proudly removed with a flourish and handed to Michael.

"What's this?" he said, peering down at the milky contents in bewilderment."

"Your favorite," she said. "Creamed peas."

He looked up in surprise to see my mom and me behind Lisa, beaming and smiling at him.

There was an awkward silence for a moment before I hurriedly jumped in and said, "Honey, I told Lisa how creamed

peas were a vegetable tradition in your family at Thanksgiving, so she made them special just for you."

"Wow," Michael said. "Thanks, Lisa—that was so sweet of you."

Later, after everyone had gone home, Michael said to me, "Honey, where'd you ever get the idea that I like creamed peas?"

"You told me!" I said.

"No, I didn't."

"Yes, you did."

"Honey, I've never eaten creamed peas in my life," Michael replied.

"Uh-huh—you told me you had them every Thanksgiving."

"You must have misunderstood," he said. "I probably said *green* peas."

"Oh."

But I couldn't tell Lisa. Not after all the hard work she'd gone to.

So for the next three Thanksgivings, Michael ate creamed peas until I finally got up the nerve to admit my mistake to my sister.

The Spirit of Christmas

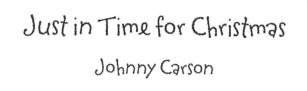

Just in Time for Christmas

Johnny Carson

Mail your packages early
so the post office can lose them
in time for Christmas.

No Wonder Jesus Loves the Little Children

Christy Ehmann

My friend's granddaughter once directed a group of four-year-olds in their Christmas pageant. Everything moved along smoothly until the children playing Mary and Joseph "arrived" at the inn in Bethlehem.

"Do you have any room for us?" asked young Joseph.

"No, the inn is full," replied the innkeeper.

"But it's so cold outside, and my wife is going to have a baby," pleaded Joseph. "Don't you have any place for us?"

To the surprise of the director and the audience, instead of showing the couple to the stable, the four-year-old innkeeper replied compassionately, "I'm not supposed to say this, but you come right on in."

An Imperfect Christmas

Dave Meurer

With candles glowing softly in the living room, snowflakes floating quietly into our front yard, and the Bible opened to that familiar "shepherds abiding" story in the Gospel of Luke, it was a picture-perfect Christmas Eve—until the coffee table erupted in flames.

In keeping with part of my German heritage, our family has always opened at least one present on the night before Christmas. Somehow a piece of wrapping paper got too close to a candle. It did not merely ignite; it exploded. I blew at it, an effort that merely slid the flaming debris off the table and into another pile of paper on the floor.

Instinctively, I began stomping on the paper in an effort to smother the flames. This is an effective way to stop a small

fire unless you happen to be wearing brand-new, furry lion's-head slippers, which will immediately flame to life like some kind of mythological beast roused from its thousand-year slumber.

In less time than it takes to sing "presents roasting on an open fire," our quiet holiday evening was transformed into a modern-day version of Dante's *Inferno*, only stupider and less poetic.

Our quiet holiday evening was transformed into a modern-day version of Dante's Inferno, only stupider and less poetic.

"Grab that thingy!" I yelled to Mark as I performed an impromptu version of "River Dance" (albeit with more smoke).

"The hose?" he yelled back.

"The red thingy that sprays stuff," I barked.

But Dale had already grabbed the fire extinguisher and began blasting away. In a roar of white mist, the flames died out and the room was filled with gently falling ashes.

We all stared quietly at the mess. My lion slippers sported melted whiskers, the coffee table bore scorch marks, and the floor was covered with a white, powdery residue belched from the extinguisher. We opened the doors and windows to clear out the smoke and spent the evening cleaning up. I don't think we ever got back to the shepherds abiding peacefully in their fields. And I finally gave up on my quest for the "perfect" Christmas.

For many years, I had embarked on a futile attempt to achieve that elusive ideal—the romanticized holiday captured in cards, magazines, and thirty-second television commercials.

The ingredients seemed so simple: a warm fire glowing in the hearth, hot cider and cinnamon sticks brewing in the kitchen, the warm flicker of candles, the glow of the tree, and my family snuggled together on the sofa as we recounted the touching story of Mary and Joseph and the baby Jesus.

But every year, something went wrong. The hearth belched smoke back into the room, a drink got spilled, the nativity-scene camel got knocked over, or one of the boys asked if he could play a video game right when the angels were about to bring tidings of great joy.

As each year passed without me realizing my dream of a perfect Christmas, I became progressively more uptight, obsessive, and ridiculous. "All I want is one perfect holiday, just one!" I complained to Dale.

"Dave, we have kids! It will *never* be perfect," Dale replied. "But can you just let it be *good?* Can you just enjoy what actually *is*, instead of what you think it *should be?*"

As is so often the case, my wife was right. It was irritating at the time, but she was right nevertheless. The perfect Christmas is a myth. After all, the first Christmas was hardly perfect. It was glorious and difficult, miraculous and earthy, sublime and sweaty, tender and harsh. Angels' songs were mixed with animals' smells. The hopes and fears of all the years were jumbled together as heaven invaded a stable.

Nothing has really changed since then. Christmas is still a mixed bag. Our hopes and fears still meet. There is the joy of the children and the aching loss in the heart of a surviving grandparent who will never again be with her beloved spouse at Christmastime. There is the uncle who will be a boor and the nephew who will be a delight. In the shallow materialism of the marketplace, hymns and carols will be played *ad infinitum* as background shopping music. And yet in the solemnity of the Christmas church service, those hymns and carols will again move us to tears, to joy, to hope.

Christmas may not be perfect. But it can be good.

Christmas without Grandma Kay

Robin Jones Gunn

"OK," I agreed with my husband, Ross. "We'll invite your family here for Christmas. But you know it's going to be hard for everyone since your mom passed away."

"I know," he said. "That's why we all need to be together." I sort of agreed with him. But I knew I couldn't take Kay's place as hostess. I was still grieving myself and didn't feel I could be responsible for the emotional atmosphere on our first holiday without her.

I made all the preparations—cookies, decorations, presents —then welcomed Ross's family on Christmas Eve with open arms as I braced myself for a holiday punctuated by sorrow.

That evening at church, our clan filled the entire back section. Afterwards, at home, the kids scampered upstairs and Ross shouted, "Five minutes!" The adults settled in the living room and Ross began to read from Luke 2.

At verse eight, our six-year-old, Rachel, appeared at the top of the stairs wearing her brother's bathrobe, a shawl over her head, and carrying a stuffed lamb under her arm. She struck a pose and stared at the light fixture over the dining-room table as if an angel had just appeared.

My father-in-law chuckled, "Look at her! You'd think she could really hear heavenly voices."

Next came Mary, one of my nieces who'd donned the blue bridesmaid dress I wore in my sister's wedding. I knew then that the kids had gotten into my closet. The plastic baby Jesus fit nicely under the full skirt of the blue dress. My son, appearing as Joseph, discreetly turned his head as Mary "brought forth" her firstborn son on the living-room floor, wrapped him in a dish towel and laid him in the laundry basket.

We heard a commotion as Ross turned to Matthew 2 and read the cue for the Magi. He repeated it, louder: "We saw His star in the east and have come to worship him."

One of my junior-high-age nephews whispered, "You go first!" and pushed his older brother out of the bedroom into full view. Slowly the ultimate wise man descended with Rachel's black tutu on his head and bearing a large bottle of canola oil.

The adults burst out laughing and I did, too, until I realized what he was wearing. It was a gold brocade dress with pearls and sequins that circled the neck and shimmered down the entire left side. Obviously the kids had gone through the bags I'd brought home after we cleaned out Kay's closet. Bags filled with shoes, hats, a few dresses, and some scarves that still smelled like her.

The laughter quickly diminished when my father-in-law said, "Hey! That's Kay's dress! What are you doing wearing her dress?"

Rachel looked at Grandpa from her perch at the top of the staircase. "Grandma doesn't mind if he uses it," she said. "I know she doesn't."

We all glanced silently at each other.

I didn't doubt that Rachel had an inside track into her grandma's heart. Kay had been there the day she was born, waiting all night in the hospital, holding a vase with two pink roses picked from her garden. She'd carried the roses through two airports and on the hour-long flight, telling everyone who she was going to see: "My son, his wife, my grandson, and the granddaughter I've been waiting for."

I'd slept with the two pink roses on my nightstand and my baby girl next to me in her bassinet. When I awoke early in the morning to nurse my squirming, squealing infant, I noticed a red mark on her cheek. Was it blood? A birthmark I hadn't noticed before?

No, it was lipstick. Grandma Kay had visited her first granddaughter sometime during the night.

It was Grandma Kay who taught Rachel the three silent squeezes. A squeeze-squeeze-squeeze of the hand means, "I love you." My first introduction to the squeezes was in the bride's dressing room on my wedding day. Kay slid past the wedding coordinator and photographer. In all the flurry, she quietly slipped her soft hand into mine and squeezed it three times. After that, I felt the silent squeezes many times. We all did.

When we got the call last year that Kay had gone into a diabetic coma, Ross caught the next plane home. Our children and I prayed this would only be a close call, like so many others the past two years. But Kay didn't come out of it this time. A week later, we tried to accept the doctor's diagnosis that it was only a matter of days. The children seemed to understand that all we could do was wait.

One night that week, Rachel couldn't sleep. I brought her to bed with me but she wouldn't settle down. She said she wanted to talk to her Grandma.

"Just have Daddy put the phone up to her ear," she pleaded. "I know she'll hear me."

It was 10:30 p.m. I called the hospital and asked for Kay's room. My husband answered at her bedside. I watched my daughter sit up straight and take a deep breath.

"OK, Rachel," my husband said. "You'll have to talk loud because there are noisy machines helping Grandma breathe."

"Grandma, it's me, Rachel!" she shouted. "I wanted to tell you good night. I'll see you in heaven."

Rachel handed me the phone and nestled down under the covers. "Oh," she said, springing up. "Tell Daddy to give Grandma three squeezes for me."

Two days later, Grandma Kay died....

Now, Christmas Eve, in our snow-covered house, Rachel was the first to welcome Grandma's memory into our celebration.

"Really, Grandpa," she continued to plead. "Grandma wouldn't mind."

We all knew Rachel was right. Grandma Kay wouldn't have cared if her grandchildren found delight in anything that belonged to her. If the dress had been embroidered with pure 14-karat gold, Grandma Kay wouldn't have minded a bit.

Grandpa nodded. The pageant continued. The next wise guy paraded down the stairs, stumbling on his too-big bathrobe and bearing a jumbo-sized Lawry's Seasoned Salt. He laid it at the laundry basket.

My husband read about the shepherds returning, "glorifying and praising God for all the things they had heard and seen, just as they had been told."

Then the cast took a bow and scrambled for the kitchen where they fought over lighting the candle on Jesus' birthday cake.

When we started singing Happy Birthday to Jesus, I looked down at the little shepherdess standing next to me.

Rachel's small, warm hand nuzzled its way into mine. I knew Grandma Kay was there, too, when I felt three silent squeezes.

We Two Kings...

Martha Bolton

How I came to be in charge of the Christmas pageant at my church that first year, I'll never know.

Whatever the reason, there I was in children's church one Sunday morning handing out parts to 30 aspiring thespians and one aspiring Donald Trump. (He somehow managed to earn a dollar from his parents for every rehearsal he made it through. I tried to get them to work out a similar deal with me, but they turned me down. They said directing the pageant would be a good learning experience for me and payment enough.)

They were right. Directing the pageant did teach me several valuable lessons. It taught me never to underestimate how fast a five-year-old can leap offstage, run down the aisle

and into Grandma's arms. It taught me never to assume that both ends of the donkey will move in the same direction. And it taught me to have plenty of Grecian Formula on hand.

In all fairness, the children didn't give me *that* much gray hair. Sure, we had the traditional pouting, crying, and "I want my mother" tantrums. But as the director, I felt entitled to do all that.

We had the usual missed cues too—like the three wise men who suddenly became a duet.

And then we faced the costume dilemma. The shepherd costume was two sizes too small, and the angel costume was big enough to cover the actor plus half of Montana. I should have fired the costume designer, but I didn't want to hurt my feelings. (Besides, sewing has never been one of my strong points. In high school, I made the only gym bag with sleeves!)

The set had its own problems. I won't go into detail, but suffice it to say that had we been doing the battle of Jericho, it would have fit perfectly.

The older children in the cast taught me a lot too. Like how to keep a straight face when they'd suggest giving the innkeeper a Mohawk haircut.

But the pageant did turn out beautifully. The children were charming, and the audience loved them. They must have loved them. So many cameras were flashing, three of the kids nearly got sunburn.

Was it worth it? Was it worth all the rehearsals, all the sleepless nights wondering if the children would wish the audience "RERMY TSIMCHRAS" instead of "MERRY CHRISTMAS" with their letter cards? Was it worth the risk of watching 30 pairs

of lips moving during "Joy to the World," but hearing only my voice? (I didn't mind taking this risk. But would the exit doors hold up under the stampede?)

Was it worth all the work, the commitment, the frazzled nerves, the late suppers, the earplugs? Yes! Because directing the Christmas pageant taught me other things as well. The innocence and the sincerity of children are refreshing, their excitement contagious. Nothing beats the feeling you get when a girl volunteers to divide her part so the new kid in the play can have some speaking lines. And years later, when I ran into a cast member who, as a young adult, still remembered his lines, I learned never to underestimate the impact a Christmas pageant can make on a young life.

So, don't worry if the ends of the donkey exit on opposite sides of the stage, or if your angel gets lost in his oversized costume. The important thing to keep sight of is what the Christmas pageant is really about—a celebration of the birth of our Lord.

A Christmas for One

Dave Meurer

The mission my wife gave me was fairly simple: Drive to the store with our two boys, Mark and Brad, and return with two strands of outdoor Christmas lights to augment our existing supply. This was another phase of her multiyear experiment in which she tried to gauge exactly how much risk she could take in sending me, and the boys, on rudimentary errands without sustaining massive economic overkill as we brought home a host of crucial items that were not on the shopping list.

Her calculations proved to be, once again, horribly flawed. You'd think she would have learned her lesson after the test in which she sent us out to buy flour and we came back with a four-person raft.

146

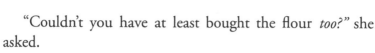

"Couldn't you have at least bought the flour *too?*" she asked.

"They were out," I replied.

"Out of flour? Dave, you went to a sporting goods store! They don't *carry* flour!"

"Well, that explains it, then," I said.

Logic is such a rare commodity today.

Our family has always loved outdoor Christmas lights. From the time our boys were very young, we have taken slow driving tours of our town at night during December. We take hot chocolate in a Thermos, wrap ourselves in blankets, roll down the car windows, and cruise through the wonderland of lights.

Our own Christmas decorating began modestly enough with a few strands of lights around a couple of windows. That wasn't enough for the kids, especially when they saw how cheap the lights were the fateful day we browsed through the aisles on our shopping mission.

"These only cost two bucks for a hundred lights," Brad whispered softly, lest any other shopper notice the great deal before we could buy out the entire aisle.

"Well, I guess we could get a few more," I said.

Mark began scooping lights off the shelf by the armful.

"Um, Mark, 'a few' does not mean 'all,'" I said. "Mom actually only wants two more strands. We can probably increase that a little, but not too much."

"But they're on *sale!* We can light up our whole house almost for free! Even the roof! And all the trees!" Mark said.

"But…" I cautioned.

"Plus, it would be fun!" Brad said.

The logic was unassailable.

We walked into the house carrying enough Christmas lights to illuminate a large metropolitan runway, or perhaps even a small nation.

Dale gasped.

"Why on earth did you buy all those lights?"

"They were out of flour," I replied.

"But…but…I didn't ask you to get flour," she stammered.

"So much the better, then," I replied.

With the enthusiastic help of the boys, I began hanging several linear miles of lights while Dale took two aspirin and a warm bath.

The result was splendid. Beautiful. Breathtaking.

It was so visually stunning that we scarcely noticed the sharp whine of the electric meter as it spun with the velocity of a buzz saw.

It was so visually stunning that we scarcely noticed the sharp whine of the electric meter as it spun with the velocity of a buzz saw. (The subsequent utility bill equaled the annual gross domestic product of Argentina. But, as Brad noted, it was fun.)

We added to the lights each year, even though Dale did not specifically request that we take on this task. On several occasions, we had to divert her attention so we could leap into the car and speed to the store before she discovered our intentions.

"Dale! Look out the back window! In the sky! Is that Haley's Comet?"

"I don't see any…" her voice trailed off as the car roared from the driveway.

The first year we moved to our current home, when Brad was ten and Mark was twelve, we again put up our light display. By this time we had enough wiring yardage to drape the windows, roof lines, chimney, garage, front fence, hedges, bushes, trees, and stray cats that walked through the yard. We even put up an outside Christmas tree and loaded it with all the remaining lights.

Dale could not walk outside at night without using sunglasses.

"Isn't this a little bit excessive?" she asked, hand on her brow to shield her eyes from the glare.

But our neighbor, an elderly woman named Millie, loved the display.

Millie was a widow and lived in the house across the street. She rarely left her home, largely because she looked after an equally aging relative who lived next door to her. She watched ministers on TV and prayed in her home because she would not leave her relative alone.

"I just love to see your lights!" Millie told Dale one day. "I look forward to it each year. I can't get out so much anymore, but I can look out my window and enjoy the sight. It makes my Christmas."

In fact, it was our Christmas light display that really sparked the friendship between Millie and Dale. It opened the door to conversations, and things took off from there. One of Millie's Christmas traditions was whipping up pounds and pounds of homemade candies, which she gave to friends and loved ones. She showered us with fudge, maple-covered walnuts, peanut brittle, and a broad array of the goodies that are so rare to youngsters today, but known so well to a generation that fades with the passing of each season.

"She *made* all this?" Mark asked as Dale brought in a tray Millie had given us.

"That must have been a ton of work," Brad said. "Why does she do it?"

"Because she loves to," Dale replied.

In the years that followed our introduction to our grandmotherly neighbor, Dale, Millie, and other ladies would occasionally get together for tea and or a visit. And Dale would pop in on Millie now and then to chat. It meant the world to Millie just to see our kids playing in the front of her house.

But as the boys grew, developing new hobbies, friends, and interests, our annual festival of lights began to dim. The boys and I would still put up lights, but fewer of them, and sometimes just days before Christmas. Life was busy, and there were just too many other things to do. It was only because Dale kept prodding us that we kept the tradition alive.

A year finally came in which Brad said, "Let's just hang a couple of strands on the fence. We live on a dead-end street, so no one even sees it except us and a couple of neighbors. Besides, it's almost Christmas, and we'll just have to take them down in a week."

I agreed, forgetting for a moment about one old, frail, sweet person.

But Dale was now leading the charge of the light brigade.

"It's important for Millie, even if no one else sees them. Please put up everything."

So Brad and I got the ladders and flashlights and trudged out into the night.

Jesus said that God notices, and rewards, small acts of thoughtfulness done in His name, even down to giving a thirsty person a glass of cold water. A glass of water may not seem like a big deal to us, but even tiny acts of service seriously matter to God.

Most of us will never be "great" as the world counts greatness. Most of us won't be in the headlines, won't be on TV, won't be in the spotlight, and won't wield great power. Odds are, most of us will scarcely be noticed outside of our small circle of family, friends, and associates.

But who we are and what we do are important to God, and no kind act will be forgotten by Him. I think one of the biggest lessons you can teach your kids is the truth that little things matter to God. And little people matter to God.

Millie passed away in the summer of 2001. Our family was at the small graveside service, which was attended by just a handful of people.

We will continue to put up our Christmas decorations, knowing that they are a pale imitation of the dazzling display Millie is enjoying now.

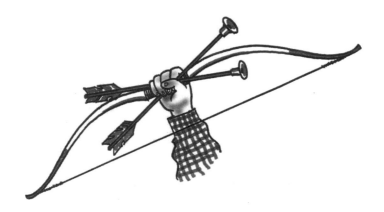

The Last Gift

Phil Callaway

The older I get, the more I'm convinced that memory and smell are linked. I close my eyes and I can almost smell Christmas. Sugar cookies baking. The turkey sizzling. I love the taste of Christmas. Mixed nuts. Mandarin oranges. Fresh dirt from one of my brother Tim's incoming snowballs. Ah, Christmastime.

When I was a child of eight or nine and Christmas was barely a week away, I sinned greatly. I sneaked into Grandpa's room, listened to him snore, then reached out and stole an entire box of chocolates, locking myself in the bathroom and eating both layers. I can still taste those chocolates. I can still feel that strap. Few sins were worth the spankings. This one

came close. It made me wonder if sometimes you're almost better off asking for forgiveness than permission.

Each December morning my sister and I would sit on a living room heat register inches from the Christmas tree, coveting toys from the Sears catalog. On the wall behind our heads, white frost had crept through the openings of an electrical outlet. Yesterday I'd earned a nickel putting my tongue on it. But otherwise I was a reasonably bright chap. The earth was somehow colder in those primitive days. Snowdrifts were higher. Winter was longer. As we sat on the heat vent, my sister pointed out certain toys in the catalog. "What do they do?" she asked. If I didn't know the answer, I made one up. "This doll's head wobbles side to side," I'd say. "Then it pops off." My sister was impressed with my knowledge.

> Each December morning my sister and I would sit on a living room heat register inches away from the Christmas tree, coveting toys from the Sears catalog.

One page in particular held a dream for me. At the top right, just above a stuffed orange bear, sat a yellow-handled bow with real suction cup arrows. "If only I could pull the wrapping off one of those," I told my sister, "my Christmas would be complete." She shook her head. "Impossible," she said. "There's no money." And when I told my brother, he agreed with my sister. "You kidding?" he laughed. "After what you did to Grandpa's chocolates? You'll be lucky to get a hand-me-down toothbrush."

Deep down I knew he was right. Deep down I dreaded Christmas. But still I shared the dream with my dad. "Ten dollars and ninety-nine cents," he winced. "You want to put us in the Poor House?" I wondered what the Poor House was like. What would we do there? Would Grandpa still come visit? Would he bring chocolates?

As December 25 drew near, I scanned the growing pile beneath the tree. Nothing. A shiny green package near the back was the right size, but late one night while everyone else slept, a flashlight informed me that the name tag was my sister's. In fact, most of them seemed to be hers. I squeezed the ones that said "Philip." They felt like practical gifts—socks, deodorant, underwear. Things you don't tell your friends about on Boxing Day.

The worst thing about Christmas morning was the waiting. My parents made us eat breakfast first. Then do the dishes. And sweep floors. And vacuum carpets. And memorize the Gospel of Luke. Then Dad prayed for the troops in Vietnam and Korea and Russia, and missionaries in countries I couldn't pronounce.

At last the time came. And this year the disappointment was overwhelming. With only three presents left beneath the tree, I held in my lap a small Tonka truck, three pairs of black socks, a shirt with pins in it, and a cowboy poster that read "When you reach the end of your rope, tie a knot in it and hang on."

The first remaining gift was a George Beverly Shea record album for my mom. The second was for Grandpa, a box of chocolates from my brother and me. The last gift was green

154

and shiny and just the right size. My sister grinned. And picked it up. Then the most unexpected thing happened: She turned and handed it to me. "Open it," she said. "It's yours. Tim put my name on it to fool you."

Mom wanted me to save the wrapping paper for next year, but it was already too late. I let out a triumphant "Whoop!" and danced around the living room, holding the bow and arrow high like the Stanley Cup. Grandpa stopped sampling chocolates and smiled widely. "It's from all of us," he said.

"You be careful with that, son," said my mother.

"He'll be okay," said my dad.

I remember only a handful of gifts from my childhood. A Detroit Red Wings hockey jersey. A Hot Wheels race car set. I remember ice-skating and carol singing and candle making, and Grandpa's story of a Baby whose tiny brow was made for thorns; whose blood would one day cleanse the world.

But it was the last gift that made Christmas come alive for me.

You see, that bow and arrow caused me to realize that Christmas is all about grace. A gift I don't deserve, coming along when I least expect it. Changing everything. Forever. "For to us a child is born, to us a son is given, and the government will be on his shoulders. And he will be called Wonderful Counselor, Mighty God, Everlasting Father, Prince of Peace" (Isaiah 9:6).

A child of eight or nine doesn't think of these things. I only knew at the time that I couldn't wait to try out the gift. I remember wolfing down turkey, my mom's special dressing, and pudding so thick you could hear it hit bottom. And I recall tiptoeing after my brother as he headed down the hallway that afternoon. I locked an arrow in place, took careful aim, and pulled on the string until it was tight.

"Hey, Tim!" I yelled. "Merry Christmas!"

And I wondered just for a moment if I should ask permission or forgiveness.

Until Next Year...

Make Every Day "Christmas"

Charles Dickens

I will honor Christmas in my heart,

and try to keep it all the year.

The Secret to Foolproof Resolutions

Karen Scalf Linamen

It's the beginning of a new year, which means it's time once again to take stock and identify changes that will make me a better person and improve the quality of my life.

I've decided to save time this year. Rather than start from scratch making my list of resolutions, I'm just going to dust off last year's list. I can do this because the same goals tend to show up year after year. For example, every single year, my list begins as follows:

Resolution Number One: Never eat anything again for the rest of my life.

I read somewhere that in the weeks between Thanks-giving and Christmas, each American gains an average of seven pounds. This tells me an awful lot of people actually lose weight over the holidays. I say this because my holiday weight gain tends to be in the triple-digit category, which means in order to end up with a national average of only seven pounds per person, some folks somewhere are drop-ping pounds big time.

The worst part about New Year's resolutions is that they are so short-lived. My wedding night negligee lasted longer than the majority of the promises I've made to myself on various January firsts throughout the years.

But I think I finally have it figured out.

I think I've finally come up with a surefire way to actually follow through with the resolutions I make this year.

Best yet, I'm going to share my secret with you. In fact, by following my instructions you, too, can wow your friends in April by announcing that you have honored your New Year's resolutions for four whole months with a flawless fervency that even Gandhi would have admired.

My secret is simply this: When you make your New Year's wish list this year, select the kinds of resolutions that you could execute successfully even if you were in a coma.

For example, this year I plan to remove, from my list, the goal of losing twenty pounds. I am going to replace it with a goal that states that no conventions attended by Elvis imper-sonators will be allowed to convene in my home during any month that ends in the letter *y*.

And you know that resolution that says I will get out of debt by eating out less often, reusing tinfoil, and making

homemade Christmas presents out of recycled dryer lint? Well, forget it. I'm going to replace that resolution with something a little more fail-safe. In fact, I've been thinking of resolving that I will never, ever allow my children to engage in science fair projects that involve the words "plastic surgery," no matter how much they beg or how many chins I have.

In fact, for even less stress and an even greater chance at success, consider resolutions such as these:

"I promise to air out the sheets on my bed by leaving it unmade whenever I am running late for work."

"I resolve to reduce my intake of sugar and fat whenever I am not currently eating sugar or fat."

"I resolve to end the new year older than I am today."

Sometimes, less is more.

> "I promise to air out the sheets on my bed by leaving it unmade whenever I am running late for work."

If I were to put a passage from the Bible on my list of New Year's resolutions, what might I choose? I could always pick the Ten Commandments, or even 1 Corinthians 13. There's no doubt about it—these verses would certainly make worthy resolutions.

But if less is more, the verse I've always loved can be found in Micah, chapter 6, verse 8. "What does the LORD require of you but to do justice, to love kindness, and to walk humbly with your God? (NASB).

Now there's a resolution that's worth its salt.

Do justice, love kindness, and walk humbly with my Lord.

Okay, I'll be the first to admit this resolution doesn't exactly fit in the category of "things you can accomplish while comatose." But you have to agree that it's not too complex. It's not unreasonable, either. Best yet, it comes with a perk or two. For starters, when I'm having a hard time following through with this resolution, the Holy Spirit is waiting to come to my assistance and help me turn these powerful words into a reality in my life. All I have to do is ask.

And when I stumble completely—when I am downright unjust, mean, and proud—Jesus is waiting to forgive and give grace.

All I have to do is ask.

What a deal!

Every January, I get frustrated because my New Year's resolutions are usually the exact same promises I made to myself the previous year. But if you ask me, these words from Micah deserve to be on my list of resolutions year after year after year.

Right next to the ban on Elvis conventions in my living room.

'Twas the Thirty Days After Christmas

Charlene Ann Baumbich

Dear First Page of My Journal,

I'm finally ready for Christmas. Shopping done. Wrapping done. Baking is as done as it's going to get—all two batches of it. House is as clean as it ever gets during the holidays.

This is the first time all season that I've had time to sit and stare at the twinkly lights of my perfectly shaped, fake Christmas tree.

At last I can take a deep breath and know that the holidays will, in spite of my procrastination and disorganization, all come together. This is the good news.

The bad news is, I'm realizing this on January 5.

January 6. I've decided to record the highlights of my day every day from now on so when bad days come I can look through your pages and be reassured that something good or exciting happens at least once every twenty-four hours.

I'm going to start this tomorrow, however, because as our grandfather clock strikes midnight, I find nothing happened today that's worth writing down except this good idea I have about writing things down.

January 7. I'd like to make the following announcement, Dear Journal: "I hereby declare myself ready to make good on my New Year's resolution to take charge of my life."

New Year's Day was supposed to be the kickoff for this transformation. But hurling myself on the couch to watch football and eat buttered popcorn with the rest of the family seemed a more giving thing to do than to selfishly isolate myself with celery sticks and devotional books. Besides, I couldn't begin my diet until the last of the Fanny Farmer Candy was gone, so I personally saw to that this morning.

I've spoken to God about the dieting dilemma—for five days running. My self-discipline is at an all-time low, although I'm sure I can chalk much of my lethargy up to sugar blues, P.M.S., and my mid-life crisis. Also, eating tastes so good.

Speaking of eating, I've got to

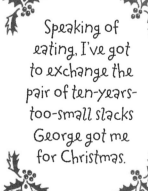

Speaking of eating, I've got to exchange the pair of ten-years-too-small slacks George got me for Christmas.

exchange the pair of ten-years-too-small slacks George got me for Christmas.

January 8. I'm embarrassed to report that the Christmas lights curled around our evergreen are still popping on at dusk, thanks to the wonders of electrical doodads that turn an ordinary switch into a timer. Seems we're the last twinklers left on our street—except, of course, the Bradleys, who never take theirs down.

Have to tell you, I'm feeling extra clever about buying three packages of slashed-price sale Christmas wrapping paper today for next Christmas. The exhilaration ranks right up there with the high I get when I manage to have dinner cooking in the crock pot by mid-morning. (Yes, Dear Journal, I am easily entertained! And see, something good does happen every day.) Too bad the dirty crock pot sometimes remains on the counter for two days before I wash it. Oh well, who'd ever want to be perfect?

January 10. Can't write much. In a rush. Promised myself that today is the day the tree is coming down! I'm beginning to fear if the house received a good shake, the dust would choke us all to death, including the parakeet, the gerbil, and my faithful dog Butch. (Wonder what a gerbil cough sounds like?)

It's not like I haven't been busy! Barb and I had a belated Christmas luncheon yesterday (whoops, oh whoops, dear calorie count). And I exchanged the slacks George gave me for some of those sand-filled weights that Velcro around your limbs. You know, extra calorie burning, extra sweat…extra pain.

January 13. I found the key ring I was going to put in Brian's stocking today. Why do I insist on hiding things every year and then forget the secret places? How did I expect to remember something hidden in a filing cabinet under "S"? Do you suppose that meant stocking? Well, at least finding it was a pleasant surprise, unlike the time I hid the chocolate bunny and found the near-white, deformed, one-eyed nightmare lurking behind the Worcestershire sauce in the cabinet above my stove.

January 15. Cloudy. Depressing. Tripping over Christmas piles of stuff that need to be boxed. I've gained two pounds and am still five days behind on my devotional reading. Like St. Paul, I wonder why I do the very things I hate…except for eating and day-dreaming which, of course, I seem to love.

And, as you already know, there just isn't time to write stuff down every day. I wish I hadn't made my January 6 promise to "record the highlights of my day every day" in ink because I could have simply erased it now instead of having to live with the falsity of my indelible words.

January 17. Let this Christmas forever go down as The Great Underwear Caper. How could I be so wrong about everyone's taste in undergarments? I've spent days exchanging my mismatched gifts.

First, I had to exchange the beautiful camisole I bought my niece—get this—for a pair of designer boxer shorts.

Next, Brian, my very own flesh and blood, was sorely disappointed I bought him Jockey Classic Briefs, which, I might add, cost a good buck. He wanted the bikini underwear that comes in a tube.

Worst of all, George snubbed his nose at the cute pair of blush-red, low-rise undies I gave to him "From Santa." He said that "at my age I'm not about to start wearing anything without a fly built into it."

(Lord, thank you for…for…instructing me not to lean on my own understanding. I don't seem to have any.)

January 20. The boxes have actually hit the attic. It's amazing how large my house seems with all the decorations down and the furniture put back in place. And I must admit it's nice to have a needle-free post holiday (Yea, fake tree!), although those pesky, prickly little things were at least a six-month reminder that Christmas really did happen.

January 24. I received the most beautiful thank you letter from Mary today. She loved, loved, loved the earrings and said they were "really her" and that it was "just like me" to find something that was "so perfect."

You know, every Christmas there seems to be one gift that I get so excited about finding. That one thing that demands the most spectacular bow. But best of all is when it's for someone like Mary whom I know will get all big-eyed and mushy about it.

(Lord, help me to be a good receiver of special gifts. To be wide-eyed and mushy—and to never forget the thank you.)

January 30. I just can't bear to part with the last trace of Christmas. The mistletoe still looks so green and inviting…I fear everyone will lose their pucker power until next year if I part with my beloved mistletoe.

My family says the magic wears off mistletoe by the end of January. I bet it lasts at least until Valentine's Day. We'll see.

February 1. The dog chewed holes in my sand bag weights yesterday. Maybe February won't be so bad after all.

Contributors

Marti Attoun has published hundreds of articles in national magazines, including *Family Circle, Ladies' Home Journal,* and *American Profile*. She lives in Joplin, Missouri.

Charlene Ann Baumbich is an author, speaker, and humorist who invites you to drop by www.dontmissyourlife.com to visit.

Martha Bolton is a former staff writer for Bob Hope, two-time Angel Award recipient, Emmy nominee, and the author of more than thirty books, including *Didn't My Skin Used to Fit?* and *Who Put the Pizza in the VCR?*

Dale Hanson Bourke is former editor of *Today's Christian Woman* magazine and the author of several books, including *Everyday Miracles: Unexpected Blessings in a Mother's Day* and *The Skeptics Guide to the Global AIDS Crisis,* and is founder of The AIDS Orphan Bracelet Project.

Phil Callaway is a popular speaker and the author of numerous bestsellers, including *Who Put the Skunk in the Trunk?* and *I Used to Have Answers, Now I Have Kids*. Visit Phil's website at www.philcallaway.ab.ca.

Patsy Clairmont, a featured speaker at Women of Faith conferences, is the author of multiple best-selling books, including *God Uses Cracked Pots, Normal Is Just a Setting on Your Dryer,* and *Sportin' a 'Tude.*

G. Ron Darbee is the author of *Nothing Builds Togetherness Like Wrestling for Remote Control* and *The Lord Is My Shepherd and I'm About to be Sheared!* His award-winning short stories have been published in a wide range of publications.

Christy Ehmann has contributed to *Today's Christian (Christian Reader)* magazine.

Chris Fabry has a variety of titles to his credit, including *Stung*, his collaboration with Jerry B. Jenkins and Dr. Tim LaHaye, and the Left Behind the Kids series. Chris has worked in Christian radio and enjoys narrating audio books as well as writing.

Debbie Farmer is an internationally syndicated newspaper columnist and author of *Don't Put Lipstick on the Cat!* (Windriver Publishing, 2003). Her essays have been published in *Reader's Digest, Family Circle,* the *Washington Post, Family Fun Magazine,* and hundreds of regional parenting magazines. Visit her website to sign up for her free e-column: www.familydaze.com.

Becky Freeman is the best-selling author of numerous titles including the best-selling *Worms in My Tea* (coauthored with her mother Ruthie Arnold), *Milk & Cookies to Make You Smile,* and *Lemonade Laughter and Laid-Back Joy.*

Robin Jones Gunn is the best-selling, award-winning author of over sixty books, including the popular Sisterchicks series. She and her husband, Ross, are the parents of two children and make their home near Portland, Oregon.

Paul M. Hampton is a pastor in western Pennsylvania, where he has served since 1988. He and his wife, Debbie, have three grown children.

Robert Hansen owns a Christmas tree farm in Chehalis, Washington, and writes a weekly humor column for the countywide *Chronicle* newspaper. A Bible-college graduate, he has formerly served as a pastor and as the director of a Christian retreat center. He and his wife, Sherry, are the parents of four children.

Jack Hayford is the senior pastor of The Church on the Way in Van Nuys, California. He is also the author of many popular books, including *The Heart of Praise.* He has composed more than four hundred hymns, worship songs, and other musical works, including the popular praise tune "Majesty."

Jana Kaumeyer is the mother of three, grandmother of four, and

wife of one. Her daughter Katy is now a mother with her own daughter, who asks her the same type of question Katy asks Jana in "A Turkey of a Dinner."

Jim Killam lives in Illinois, where he teaches college journalism and is a freelance writer.

Tina Krause is a newspaper columnist, mother, and the author of *Laughter Therapy: A Dose of Humor for the Christian Woman's Heart.*

Karen Scalf Linamen is the author of numerous books, including *Welcome to the Funny Farm* and *I'm Not Suffering from Insanity . . . I'm Enjoying Every Minute of It!* She is the author of more than one hundred magazine articles and speaks frequently at churches, women's retreats, and writers' conferences.

Mary Wanda Little, age eighty, is the mother of three children and the grandmother of seven. For the past fifty-two years she has been, and continues, writing and editing the monthly newsletter of her local Presbyterian church, in McConnelsville, Ohio.

Dave Meurer is the author of several books, including *Good Spousekeeping* and *If You Want Breakfast in Bed, Sleep in the Kitchen.* He is the winner of numerous state and national writing awards and honors. His writings have appeared in such major publications as *Focus on the Family* and *Homelife.*

Lynn Bowen Walker is a freelance writer whose work has appeared in numerous periodicals, including *Today's Christian Woman, Christian Parenting Today, Glamour,* and *American Baby.* Lynn is also the author of *Queen of the Castle: 52 Weeks of Homemaking Encouragement for the Uninspired, Domestically Challenged, or Just Plain Tired.* She and her husband, Mark, are the parents of two sons.

Laura Jensen Walker is a popular public speaker and author whose works include *A Kiss Is Still a Kiss, Through the Rocky Road and Into the Rainbow Sherbet, Love Handles for the Romantically Impaired* and her first novel, *Dreaming in Black and White.*

C. Ellen Watts writes regularly for Christian and inspirational markets. Her books include *Over 60 and Picking Up Speed.* While she has an effervescent and lovable supply of grands and greats, she finds time to mentor young writers and has two books in progress.

Tim Wildmon is president of the American Family Association, a Christian organization based in Tupelo, Mississippi. He and his wife, Alison, are the parents of three children.

171

Source Notes

Chapter 1: Christmas Is Coming, Tra-La, Tra-La

"All I Want for Christmas Is a Parking Place" by Dave Barry.

"The Best-Laid Plans" is taken from *Welcome to the Funny Farm* by Karen Scalf Linamen, Revell Books, a division of Baker Publishing Group, copyright © 2001. Used by permission of Baker Publishing Group.

"Thanksgiving Rolls Around, and So Do the Dishes" by Marti Attoun. Used by permission.

"A Thanksgiving Recipe" taken from *The Lord Is My Shepherd* by G. Ron Darbee. Copyright © 1998. Used by permission.

"Who Needs Cookbooks When You've Got a Phone?" by Marti Attoun. Used by permission.

"On Wings Like Turkeys" taken from *At the Corner of Mundane and Grace* by Chris Fabry. WaterBrook Press, a division of Random House, Inc., Colorado Springs, CO. Copyright © 1999.

"Fowl Play! (How Not to Be a Turkey at the Thanksgiving Table)" by Marti Attoun. Used by permission.

"When You Need a Little Christmas...*Now*" taken from *Marriage 911* by Becky Freeman. Copyright © 1996. Used by permission.

"Shop 'Til You Drop" is taken from *Welcome to the Funny Farm* by Karen Scalf Linamen, Revell Books, a division of Baker Publishing Group, copyright © 2001. Used by permission of Baker Publishing Group.

Chapter 2: The Chaos Theory of Christmas

"But Can She Drive a Sleigh?" by Shirley Temple.

"Christmas, a Labor of Love" is taken from *Welcome to the Funny Farm* by Karen Scalf Linamen, Revell Books, a division of Baker Publishing Group, copyright © 2001. Used by permission of Baker Publishing Group.

"Lights, Camera...Too Much Action" by Jim Killam. Used by permission.

"A So-Called Tree and Thee" taken from *Mama Said There'd Be Days Like This* by Charlene Ann Baumbich. Copyright © 1995. Used by permission.

"Dear Santa" by Debbie Farmer, taken from *Amazing Grace for Mothers: 101 Stories of Faith, Hope, Inspiration & Humor* by Emily Cavins and Patti Armstrong with Jeff Cavins and Matthew Pinto. Copyright © 2004. Ascension Press, West Chester, PA.

"Merry Christmas (with Cramps)" taken from *Come . . . and Behold Him* by Jack Hayford. Multnomah Publishers, 1995. Used by permission.

"Are You *Sure* the Wise Men Wore Turtlenecks?" is taken from *If Mr. Clean Calls, Tell Him I'm Not In* by Martha Bolton, Revell Books, a division of Baker Publishing Group, copyright © 2000. Used by permission of Baker Publishing Group.

"It's Beginning to Feel a Lot Like Christmas" is taken from *Welcome to the Funny Farm* by Karen Scalf Linamen, Revell Books, a division of Baker Publishing Group, copyright © 2001. Used by permission of Baker Publishing Group.

"See Mother, Funny, Funny Mother," Author unknown.

Chapter 3: The Gift of Christmas

"Separating the Men from the Boys" by Lee Daniel Quinn.

"Things Never to Give Your Wife for Christmas" © 1995 by Honor

Books. *The Greatest Christmas Ever.* Used with permission by Cook Communications Ministries. May not be further reproduced. To order, call 1-800-323-7543 or online www.cookministries.com. All rights reserved.

"Things Never to Give Your Husband for Christmas" © 1995 by Honor Books. *The Greatest Christmas Ever.* Used with permission by Cook Communications Ministries. May not be further reproduced. To order, call 1-800-323-7543 or online www.cookministries.com. All rights reserved.

"Don't Look a Gift Horse in the Slippers" by Lynn Bowen Walker. Used by permission.

"What Goes Up Must Come Down" taken from *Who Put the Pizza in the VCR?* by Martha Bolton, published by Vine Books, a division of Servant Publications. Copyright © 1996 by Martha Bolton. Used with permission.

"The Gift That Keeps on Giving (Unfortunately)" © 2005 by Dave Meurer. *If You Want Breakfast in Bed, Sleep in the Kitchen.* Used with permission by Cook Communications Ministries. May not be further reproduced. To order, call 1-800-323-7543 or online www.cookministries.com. All rights reserved.

"Christmas Shenanigans" by Robert Hansen. Permission granted to include a portion of *Why Can't Women Understand Men? We're So Simple* by Robert Hansen, AMG Publishers, Chattanooga, TN, © 2002.

"Show Me the Money" by C. Ellen Watts first appeared as "Kids of the Kingdom" in the November/December 2000 issue of *Today's Christian* (formerly *Christian Reader*), a publication of Christianity Today, Inc. Used by permission.

"Gifts That Make Mom a Packrat" is taken from *The "Official" Mom Book* by Martha Bolton, published by Howard Publishing Co., Inc. Copyright © 2004. Used by permission.

"Putting the 'X' in X-mas" by Paul M. Hampton first appeared in the January/February 1998 issue of *Today's Christian* (formerly *Christian Reader*), a publication of Christianity Today, Inc. Used by permission.

"Gifts that Keep on Giving (Me a Headache)" taken from *Normal Is Just a Setting on Your Dryer* (chapter originally titled "Crafty"), a Focus on the Family book published by Tyndale House Publishers. Copyright © 1993 by Patsy Clairmont. All rights reserved. International copyright secured. Used by permission.

"Some Assembly Required (and a Little Prozac Wouldn't Hurt Either)" is taken from *If Mr. Clean Calls, Tell Him I'm Not In* by Martha

Bolton, Revell Books, a division of Baker Publishing Group, copyright © 2000. Used by permission of Baker Publishing Group.

"Gift-Giving Misgivings" from *My Life as a Half-Baked Christian* by Tim Wildmon, published by Barbour Books, an imprint of Barbour Publishing, Inc., Uhrichsville, Ohio. Used by permission.

Chapter 4: Peas on Earth... and Other Tasty Holiday Tidbits

"Good Stuffings," Author unknown.

"All Fired Up for the Ladies' Christmas Coffee" is taken from *Help! I'm Turning Into My Mother.* Copyright © 2002 by Becky Freeman and Ruthie Arnold. Published by Harvest House Publishers, Eugene, OR. Used by permission. www.harvesthousepublishers.com.

"A Turkey of a Dinner" by Jana Kaumeyer first appeared in the November/December 1996 issue of *Today's Christian* (formerly *Christian Reader*), a publication of Christianity Today, Inc. Used by permission.

"Where's the Fire?" taken from *Who Put the Pizza in the VCR?* by Martha Bolton, published by Vine Books, a division of Servant Publications. Copyright © 1996 by Martha Bolton. Used with permission.

"Baking Cookies? Bah! Humbug!" from *Laughter Therapy* by Tina Krause, published by Barbour Books, an imprint of Barbour Publishing, Inc., Uhrichsville, Ohio, 2002. Used by permission.

"'Tis the Season" taken from *Nothing Builds Togetherness Like Wrestling for Remote Control* by G. Ron Darbee. Copyright © 1996. Used by permission.

"Holiday Memories," copyright © 1984 by Dale Hanson Bourke. Used by permission. This story may not be reprinted without permission of the author.

"Is the Turkey Burned Yet?" taken from *If You Can't Stand the Smoke, Stay Out of My Kitchen* by Martha Bolton. Copyright © 1990. Published by Beacon Hill Press of Kansas City. All rights reserved. Used by permission.

"The Call of the Popcorn" taken from *Worms in My Tea* by Becky Freeman and Ruthie Arnold. Copyright © 1994. Used by permission.

"When Is a Leg Like an Ear?" by Mary Wanda Little first appeared in the November/December 1999 issue of *Today's Christian* (formerly *Christian Reader*), a publication of Christianity Today, Inc. Used by permission.

"Let There Be Peas on Earth" is taken from *Love Handles for the Romantically Impaired* by Laura Jensen Walker, Revell Books, a division of Baker Publishing Group, copyright © 2002. Used by permission of Baker Publishing Group.

Chapter 5: The Spirit of Christmas

"Just in Time for Christmas" by Johnny Carson.

"No Wonder Jesus Loves the Little Children" by Christy Ehmann first appeared in the November/December 1998 issue of *Today's Christian* (formerly *Christian Reader*), a publication of Christianity Today, Inc.

"An Imperfect Christmas" © 2005 by Dave Meurer. *Good Spousekeeping.* Used with permission by Cook Communications Ministries. May not be further reproduced. To order, call 1-800-323-7543 or online www.cookministries.com. All rights reserved.

"Christmas without Grandma Kay" by Robin Jones Gunn. Used by permission.

"We Two Kings…" taken from *If You Can't Stand the Smoke, Stay Out of My Kitchen* by Martha Bolton. Copyright © 1990. Published by Beacon Hill Press of Kansas City. All rights reserved. Used by permission.

"A Christmas for One" is taken from *Stark Raving Dad* by Dave Meurer, Revell Books, a division of Baker Publishing Group, copyright © 2005. Used by permission of Baker Publishing Group.

"The Last Gift" is taken from *Who Put My Life on Fast-Forward?* Copyright © 2002 by Phil Callaway. Published by Harvest House Publishers, Eugene, OR. Used by permission. www.harvesthousepublishers.com

Chapter 6: Until Next Year…

"Make Every Day 'Christmas' " by Charles Dickens. Public domain.

"The Secret to Foolproof Resolutions" is taken from *Welcome to the Funny Farm* by Karen Scalf Linamen, Revell Books, a division of Baker Publishing Group, copyright © 2001. Used by permission of Baker Publishing Group.

"'Twas the Thirty Days after Christmas" taken from *Mama Said There'd Be Days Like This* by Charlene Ann Baumbich. Copyright © 1995. Used by permission.